HOW TO CALIFORNIA

Jonathan Roberts

D1594088

Photographs by Bob Ware
Design by Charles Kreloff

A DELL TRADE PAPERBACK

A DELL TRADE PAPERBACK

Published by
Dell Publishing Co., Inc.
1 Dag Hammarskjold Plaza
New York, New York 10017

Dell ® TM 681510, Dell Publishing Co., Inc.

Printed in the United States of America

First printing—July 1984

Library of Congress Cataloging in
Publication Data

Roberts, Jonathan.
    How to California.
    1. California—Social life and
customs—Anecdotes,
facetiae, satire, etc.   I. Title.
F866.2.R63   1984   306'.09794
84-4221
ISBN 0-440-53366-X

Have a nice day.

Acknowledgments

Books like this—concept books—are intended to look casual and effortless. But almost invariably, they exist only because a network of friends, acquaintances, and contacts (which is what friends and acquaintances are called in The Industry) provided a full range of support services.

The network behind *How to California* starts with three editors: Morgan Entrekin, who bought me that first sushi lunch over which we thought of the idea in the first place and who saw the book through its childhood; Susan Moldow, who came to the project in its difficult adolescent years and brought wit and sense to it; and Gary Luke, who worked so diligently to create the illusion that the book was finally full grown.

My old friend and colleague Charles Kreloff brought his perfect blend of professionalism and inspiration to the art direction of the book, and Bob Ware, throughout as harrowing a work schedule as could be dumped on a photographer, maintained an unfailingly creative eye and never lost his patience (or his puns).

Charlotte Sheedy, my agent, has always responded with warmth and wisdom to more than the standard percentage of problems from me, and I am grateful.

The biggest part of the network is made up of people who gave information, ideas, advice, and special observations on all the subjects covered in *How to California*; also, people who provided services, props, locations, and technical help; and of course people who risked ridicule by modeling. They include Tom Alrick, Matt Bedrosian, Gladyce Begelman, Shelly Berger, Alan Berliner, Ruth Berliner, Paul Bilsky, Roger Birnbaum, Susan Blond (who was with me the first time I got paged), Steve Bloom,

Annie Brody, Jim Brown, John Burnham, Andy and Gayle Carmichael (who for that first week *were* Southern California for me), James Cassimus, Douglas Crockett, Jeri Cummins, Sean Daly, Andrea Davis, Andrew Davis, Greg DeSantis, Katy Dobbs, Lex duPont, Laurance duPont, Davis Factor, Dean Factor, the completely wonderful Janet Factor, Bruce Feirstein, Helene and Jim Feuerstein, Jon Gould (a friend for both coasts), Jackson Harvey, Tony Hendra, Brian Ingram, Ish from A & I Color Laboratory, Alison Jackson, Laurette Kite, Randie Laine, Andrew Laurence, Terry Lee, Jeff Levy, Maggie Lichota, Steven Lippman, Gail MacColl, Malcolm McAlpine, Margaux's Drive-A-Dream Division of Budget Rent-A-Car of Beverly Hills, Jessica Montaigne, D. David Morin (that rare blend—suave *and* intelligent), Rob Reiner, Susan Reu, Eileen Roaman, Jennifer Rogers, Sandy's Ski & Sports, Andy Scheinman, Peggy Siegel, Celia Smith, Garrett Stewart, John Stockwell, Nancy Stone, Tom Styron, Patrick Terrail, Carol Wallace, Andy Warhol, Nancy Wechsler, Mason Wiley, Richard Wright, Robin Wright, and Cindy Zurawski.

To all of these people, and to any who were inadvertently omitted, I am very, very grateful.

JSR

Contents

Introduction

Congratulations.

Simply by picking up this copy of How to California *you have moved one step closer to the life you always saw on television but never before dreamed you could have as your own.*

And if you study this book carefully, in eleven short weeks—about as long as the good weather lasts where most of you reside—you can live the way people do where the weather is great all year round.

No matter where you are. That's right. California in Kalamazoo.

Sounds hard to believe, doesn't it? For sure. But I did it. And if I could do it, so can you. I know. I was once like you.

I lived in a place where it snowed in the winter. Where if you wanted to get someplace, you often went by foot, or by bus or train. Where the oranges were brought in from far away. Where nobody wore a bathing suit to the bank, and where they only had one kind of sprout in the supermarket. And sometimes not even that.

I thought Southern California was a made-for-TV sort of place. I thought perfect weather was a stupid idea. I thought surfing was done by trick photography. I thought Southern California was . . . well, silly.

But I had this nagging doubt: If it's so silly, why does it seem like so much fun? I had to find out. I moved to Southern California. I watched, and studied, and made notes. I learned how to California.

Now I live like a Southern Californian even when I'm not in Southern California. I wear sunglasses. I drive everywhere. I have a tan. I have a nice day.

My life has been transformed.

And these observations and notes grew into the eleven-week course upon which you are about to embark.

An explanation—a few of you are already grumbling. "But what about Northern California? This book is only about Southern California, and only certain aspects of it, at that. How can it be called simply How to California?*" Easy. This book is about the California that springs to mind when most of us think "California." (Or at least when I do.) If you don't like that California, hey, that's cool. But don't expect not to be confronted by it when you watch a TV series or a talk show, or read any self-respecting trash novel or gossip magazine. Face it. A lot of America is fascinated by that California.*

So here it is, pandering to your base instincts to live at the end of the rainbow.

Have a nice day.

Week 1

CARS

After sleeping, which takes up one third of our time, and working, which takes up a bit less, driving is the most time-consuming activity of the Southern Californian. More time-consuming than eating, more time-consuming than sex, even more time-consuming than jogging, tanning, and est put together.

While driving, Californians do things that other Americans would do in their bathrooms, bedrooms, offices, dining rooms, dressing rooms, or gymnasiums. For this reason a Californian's car is especially important to him, and if the abundance of expensive and well-maintained cars here seems at first astonishing, it is due only partly to the great wealth here. In equal measure it is due to drivers' (which is synonymous with Southern Californians') putting a greater share of their incomes, personalities, thought, and all-around effort into their cars. Cars, after all, outlast jobs, earthquakes, divorces, and often car owners.

Before you buy your car in Southern California, think very carefully. Read this chapter. Ask yourself, "What kind of car says me?" Please believe this is not a ridiculous question. You will be judged—and judged very carefully—by what you drive.

Only you can decide if you are a Pinto, or a Rolls. If you want to brand yourself as an outsider to Southern California, nothing will work faster than to utter the great cliché, "Everybody drives everywhere here." The true Californian responds, "Yeah, so?"

The correct remark is "What do you drive?"

That is the question in Southern California. What you drive is infinitely more interesting than that you drive. You are, after all, known by what you drive.

"You remember her, don't you?"

"No."

"Sure you do. She drove that blue Fiat 124."

"Oh, her. Of course!"

As a service to help you better remember people, here is the official breakdown of Who Drives What (arranged by car, of course), along with the essential identifying marks of the first accessory that must be purchased for each car, and the message on the license-plate frame.

BMW

Driven by: The BMW 318i (the smaller coupe) is driven by a young record company executive or a young William Morris agent. Depending on which, there are always either press releases or scripts all over the back seat. The 733i (four-door sedan) is for the family man who is fond of saying at parties that he doesn't own a Mercedes because he is more interested in what's *under* the hood than what's *on* the hood. He got this idea from a BMW ad. The BMW 633CSi (the fancier coupe) is for the older record executive or agent. There is nothing in the back seat, but the agent has a phone in the front.

First accessory: Brake covers to collect the black brake dust that discolors the rims (front wheels only).

License-plate frame reads: ZIPPER BMW/BEVERLY HILLS.

9

CADILLAC

Driven by: Successful people over fifty. The big models—the Fleetwood and the De Ville—are for Palm Springs residents. They are rich enough to afford a more expensive car, but find the Caddy the most appropriate complement to big platinum hairdos (women) and crew cuts and golf ensembles (men). Rich Retirees is the phrase to remember here. The Seville is the

cosmopolitan Caddy, popular with doctors' wives.

First accessory: Curb feelers.

License-plate frame reads: USC ALUMNI.

CHEVROLET IMPALA SEDAN (CIRCA 1973)

Driven by: Chicano family.

First Accessory: Window fringe.

License-plate frame reads: (Lowered suspension has caused frame to snap off).

CORVETTE

Driven by: Over forty and single. A real swinger. Shoes match belt.

First accessory: Eight-track stereo with Kenny Rogers tape.

License-plate frame reads: DAMN, I'M GOOD!

JEEP CJ

Driven by: Originally, Marlboro men and Colorado types; next, Beverly Hills High students; now, gay men into the high-tech look.

First accessory: All-black paint job.

License-plate frame reads: SO MANY MEN . . . SO LITTLE TIME.

DATSUN ZX MODELS

Driven by: Stewardesses. Seen frequently in Marina Del Rey, especially in metallic colors, especially with automatic transmissions. This is a luxury car posing as a sports car, and it is also popular with the recently divorced person, posing as a suave swingle. The marginally hipper stewardess or divorcée drives a Mazda RX-7.

First accessory: Z-related vanity plate (see "ELP Yourself")

License-plate frame reads: HAPPINESS IS BEING SINGLE.

HONDA PRELUDE

Driven by: Cheerleader who received car as sweet-sixteen gift.

First accessory: Boyfriend.

License-plate frame reads: EASY DOES IT.

SAAB TURBO

Driven by: Rich skier.

First accessory: Condo at Mammoth Mountain.

License-plate frame reads: SKIERS GO DOWN FASTER.

VAN

Driven by: What sort of man reads *Playboy*? That's the desired image; actually the car is driven by a male high school student who can't have sex at home.

First accessory: Full conversion, including free-form bubble window, shag carpeting for walls, floor, and ceiling; mattress, mag wheels, and the loudest possible stereo.

License-plate frame reads: IF MY VAN'S A-ROCKIN'/DON'T COME KNOCKIN'.

MERCEDES SL

Driven by: Successful people under fifty. The Mercedes SL's are the all-time basic Southern California status-symbol cars. They are the two-door, two-seater models with the choice of a removable hardtop or a convertible roof. The current model is the 380SL (the number is for the engine size), which is directly descended from a proud line of status symbols. Before the 380SL was the 450SL, and before that was the 350SL, preceded by (in reverse order) the 280SL, the 250SL, the 230SL, the 190SL, and so forth. This litany is important; it is part of the received wisdom passed down among the schoolchildren of Beverly Hills.

First accessory: Nardi steering wheel (slightly smaller than stock wheel).

License-plate frame reads: MERCEDES-BENZ (just as an extra reminder).

(The other Mercedes models have more specialized purposes. The SLC coupe [a hard-top four-seater two-door] is the older people's SL, affording security to those afraid of soft tops. The Turbo Diesel sedan is the favorite of rich Asian families. The 380SEL sedan is for people who "absolutely need this car" for their business. For real estate agents, this is probably true. And the Mercedes station wagon is for practitioners of California's special idea of reverse snobbery. The principle is this: A station wagon is so practical that a thirty-five thousand dollar station wagon must be twenty-five thousand more practical than a Ford Country Squire.)

PONTIAC TRANS AM

Driven by: Iranian student.

First accessory: Huge flaming phoenix decal on hood.

License-plate frame reads: USC TROJANS.

FOUR-BY-FOUR (PICKUP CONVERTED FOR OFF-ROAD DRIVING)

Driven by: Male up to age twenty-two, long hair. If in school, cuts classes. Puts stickers advertising heavy-metal bands in window, dirt bike in back. Calls driving off-road "bouncing."

First accessory: Ladder, in order to reach cab after installation of suspension high enough to clear a Volkswagen.

License-plate frame reads: GRASS, GAS, OR ASS . . . NO ONE RIDES FOR FREE or NO FAT CHICKS.

PORSCHE

Driven by: The 911 is driven by young lawyers. The 911 Turbo is driven by doctors. The Targa—that's the one with the pop-off roof—raises a special problem. There is a snobbery among the ranks of Porsche owners which suggests that while the Targa is superficially more fun, the true Porsche lover will insist on the basic 911 coupe body, which he or she maintains has more structural integrity. Targa lovers deny that there is any significant difference. And they have better tans.

The Porsche 924—the least expensive model—is generally dismissed as "just a fancy Audi" by owners of fancier Porsches, who see it as a Porsche with training wheels. It is a first step into the Porsche world for many drivers, however, and deserves some affection as Baby's First Porsche. It has been replaced by the 944, but it will be a few years before the new model settles into its niche.

The 928—that's the really exotic forty-thousand-dollar one with the headlights that point straight upward when at rest—is also popular with the first-time Porsche owners. That is, with the especially rich first-timers. Also, it has room for a couple of kids in back, which attracts the married crowd. The owners of the more classic 911 series cars say, "It's a great car, sure. But I mean, it's not a *Porsche,* if you know what I mean." Other 911 owners know exactly what they mean.

First accessory: Ignition key with built-in flashlight. On the Turbo the first accessory is a Blaupunkt stereo with a remote tuning console on the end of a gooseneck so you don't have to reach all the way to the dashboard to change stations. A Blaupunkt is also the second accessory, when the first gets ripped off.

License-plate frame reads: PORSCHE (same rationale as Mercedes—you can never have too much of a good thing).

VW BUS (IN RUNNING ORDER)

Driven by: Surfer.

First accessory: Bumper sticker reading HUSSONG'S CANTINA, ENSENADA.

License-plate frame reads: TOURISTS GO HOME ... BUT LEAVE YOUR DAUGHTERS.

VW BUS (NOT IN RUNNING ORDER)

Driven by: Hippie.

First accessory: Bumper sticker reading ONE PLANET, ONE PEOPLE ... PLEASE.

License-plate frame reads: MY OTHER CAR IS SOLAR.

VW BUG CONVERTIBLE

Driven by: Almost anyone, but especially the California Girl. It's the perfect California car: expensive enough to be respectable, open to the sun, spunky, totally hip. The California Girl has the top down and is always just out of reach on the highway. As the old bug convertibles disappear from the roads, they are replaced by Rabbit Convertibles.

First accessory: Tennis visor hat.

License-plate frame reads: HONOLULU VOLKSWAGEN.

THE VW RABBIT CONVERTIBLE

Driven by: Beverly Hills High School students. While not exactly the car of choice among this group (that position is reserved for Porsche and Mercedes), it is certainly the *likeliest* car given to one by daddy as a reward for passing the grueling driver's license exam. And at eleven or twelve thousand dollars, it makes a much more appropriate gift for a mere teen-ager.

First accessory: Cigarettes.

License-plate frame reads: PRECISION MOTORS, BEVERLY HILLS.

VW RABBIT GTI

Driven by: Undercover Porsche driver who doesn't want you to notice that he's about to blow you away, pulling away from that traffic light.

First accessory: Radar detector.

License-plate frame reads: (car moving too fast to read).

VOLKSWAGEN SCIROCCO

Driven by: College student. This is the college student's Porsche. Except at USC, where the Porsche is the college student's Porsche.

First accessory: Front-end air dam.

License-plate frame reads: MY OTHER CAR IS A PORSCHE.

Off the High End

"High-end cars" is a euphemism particularly apt to Southern California. It is dealers' lingo for cars that cost in the area of, say, sixty-five thousand dollars and up. If the term sounds a little too casual to the rest of the country, it should be remembered that in Southern California such cars are actually commonplace; there are neighborhoods where there are Rolls-Royces parked in front of a good half of the houses. In simpler terms, sixty-five-thousand-dollar cars are a dime a dozen out here, if that dime is a rare, misstruck coin worth $780,000.

Owning a high-end car isn't so tough, really, assuming you can afford it, and only slightly more difficult assuming you can't afford it. (In that case you may find comfort in knowing that Southern California car financing surpasses the movie industry for creativity.) There are only a few cardinal rules:

1. Have something else to drive just in case, and expect one case per month. Don't worry if you don't know your mechanic very well. You will.
2. Take up two spaces, everywhere. Don't worry. People don't resent it here—they *understand.*
3. The AAA has flatbed trucks available for high-end cars stuck on the road. Never let them send an ordinary tow truck. Not so much because that might damage your car, but because a flatbed really displays the car to its best advantage.
4. Keep it clean.

Rich Southern Californians are proud of their money; more so than anyone except perhaps Texans. Still, social convention requires that in conversation they be prepared to rationalize their choice of a high-end car—if only as a way of turning conversation to themselves. In this spirit, then, here is a selection of high-end cars, and high-end rationales.

ROLLS-ROYCE $110,000 AND UP

Rationale: Face it, The Rolls-Royce is all about money.

Merv drives a Rolls.

The Rolls is the only car that consistently pulls the stares of rubberneckers. *Everyone* wants to know who's driving the Rolls.

The flying-lady hood ornament—properly called the Spirit of Ecstasy—is occasionally stolen. A new one costs $580 from the dealer. The California Sales Tax is $38.40. This does not include labor.

So what is your rationale? Simple. You buy a 1974 or 1975 Rolls-Royce Silver Shadow. It looks just like the 1980 model, and costs far less. You are being *economical.*

Dealers of high-end cars will admit to being impressed by anyone who buys a Rolls Corniche—the two-door coupe or convertible. These people aren't just stretching their budgets; they have actually tapped the wellspring of the petrodollars. A Corniche convertible costs $163,500, if you include the optional $500 right-hand mirror.

The rationale for the Corniche is that you already have a four-door car. There is no rationale for the mirror.

There is a newer Rolls sedan, called the Silver Spirit. It looks just like a Volvo, only bigger. The rationale is that you wanted a sensible Volvo, but were concerned for the safety of your family, riding in such a small car.

EXCALIBUR

Rationale: You're old fashioned at heart, really you are, and what could warm every fiber of your soul better than a nearly exact Fiberglas replica of a 1920s Mercedes SSK Roadster? Fifty thousand dollars will buy you just that, with a handy GM engine and transmission as part of the bargain.

The historical purist in you will quietly replace the Excalibur hood ornament (a sword) with a Mercedes crest (an emasculated peace symbol).

CLENET (RHYMES WITH B'NAI) CABRIOLET

Rationale: It's what to buy when your next-door neighbor buys an Excalibur, because a Clenet costs $80,000. Not exactly a replica (or *replicar,* as the genre is called) but a roadster with a rakish "1930s look" nonetheless: swooping clamshell fenders, etched glass windows, and all.

If some of that "1930s look" is a vaguely *familiar* look, it is with good reason. The car's cowl—the doors, windows, windshield, and roof—is constructed from stock Volkswagen Beetle convertible body parts. All this is served up on a Lincoln-Mercury chassis, making repairs as easy as, say, getting a Lincoln or Mercury fixed.

FERRARI

The rationale for Ferraris is that a pair of them does wonders for a marriage. Traditionally the husband gets a Berlinetta Boxer 512. Its flat five-liter twelve-cylinder engine gives it a top speed of 188 miles per hour, which is very comforting news. This car must be *homologated* upon its arrival in the USA, which means sending it to a sort of reform school for cars where it is trained to meet U.S. Department of Transportation legal standards. You will buy this in red.

The wife gets the Ferrari 400i automatic. It, too, has a

V-12 engine, which can be understood by imagining a car being pulled by three Toyotas, all going 175 miles per hour. The car seats four, and you will buy it in black.

LAMBORGHINI COUNTACH (RHYMES WITH PRUNE DASH)

That you are interested in the space program is as good a rationale as any for owning the Countach, since it truly looks like a spaceship. It is all aluminum, and its flat twelve-cylinder engine develops 375 horsepower, giving it a rumored top speed of 207 miles per hour. It costs around $100,000 to $120,000, or about five hundred dollars per mile per hour.

A tight parking space might be another good rationale, as the Countach's doors swivel straight up into the air.

Rod Stewart drove one to his Sunday-morning soccer games on Coldwater Canyon Drive.

The Rolex Drape

Southern California Time is generally displayed on a Rolex watch, and to do it right, the Rolex itself must be properly displayed, too.

In The Industry, among the super-rich, among the semi–super-rich and among those wishing to appear to belong to any of those categories, the all-gold $8,700 Rolex President watch is as necessary a part of the proper uniform as a hard hat in a coal mine or a suit and tie on Wall Street. In fact in certain business settings, such as around the pool at the Beverly Hills Hotel, it is very nearly the *only* thing worn and it still has the power to say "power." When they bring that martini-olive-green extension phone to your chaise longue because you've just arranged to have yourself paged poolside, you must remember to reach for the receiver with your left hand, because that's the one with the Rolex. The newly engaged woman who finds a thousand reasons to display her diamond ring doesn't hold a candle to the display of candlepower glinting off the oft-raised wrist of the new (or even long-term) Rolex President wearer.

But there is one way of displaying the Rolex that outshines all the others, both for flash and for popularity. It is the *Rolex drape,* and you can do it yourself with these simple instructions.

Get yourself a Rolls-Royce or, if you must, one of the more expensive Mercedes models. Position yourself behind the steering wheel, wearing the Rolex on your left wrist.

Open the driver's side window.

Place the inside of your left wrist on top of the steering wheel, at about the ten or eleven o'clock position. Relax the wrist so that the hand *drapes* over the wheel. You will need to grip the wheel with your right hand, in order to steer. *The left hand must not* grip the wheel; only the position described above will permit the *Rolex to be exhibited at the absolute apex of the forearm/wheel juncture.*

Drive up and down Rodeo Drive, or Wilshire Boulevard near Rodeo Drive. Go slowly.

Do not look to the right or left. You *must have confidence* that the driver next to you is noticing. Unless, of course, he is doing his own Rolex drape.

The VW Cult

A worried reader inquires, "I'm a little short of cash just now. You know, waiting for residuals to come in from syndication and all. What should I drive? I still need to be cool."

Worried Reader will be comforted to know that there is a cheap and easy solution to the problem.

The VW Beetle.

First of all, it's not made anymore, so it's at least a semiclassic. Secondly, with its clamshell fenders and running boards, it may even be a true classic.

It costs very little, unless it has been elaborately modified, in which case it's probably not for sale anyway, because the owner intends to keep it forever. There is tremendous competition in the field of independent VW repair, ensuring relatively low maintenance costs. Most repairs can be done at home, and even changing the engine entirely is common practice. With a couple of decades' worth of essentially identical VW Beetles on the road, there is a ready supply of parts, ensuring a long life for your car.

There are two special categories of Beetle which are found almost exclusively in California. The Baja Bug is a modified Beetle, with specially designed shorter front and rear ends substituted. The engine is exposed, the suspension is raised, huge balloon tires are added, making the Baja Bug into a sort of Teutonic dune buggy. You must only get or make a Baja Bug if you are male and within your first eight years of driving.

The other special category to be named for California: the Cal Look Bug. This is a process of painting or replacing all exterior chrome trim so that it has a matte black finish. The chrome-accented rubber seals around the windows are replaced with all-rubber seals. There is no reason for this. It just looks cool. If you don't believe it, just pick up a copy of *Hot VWs* magazine, a staple of any Southern California newsstand, specializing in all manner of modified VWs.

The VW Karmann Ghia sports car and the VW Beetle convertible are fully cool, too, but they are also fully expensive.

Going Topless

I n Southern California the convertible is *not* dead.

It is *always* desirable to own a convertible. The convertible owner *always* has more fun. There is no such thing as an uncool convertible. Even a model that would otherwise be tacky, undesirable, or ridiculous—a late-sixties Dodge Dart, for example—becomes acceptable and even fashionable in the convertible model.

California is the *locus classicus* of custom convertibles—conversions of hardtop cars to soft. Anything from a Cadillac Seville to a garden variety Toyota can and will be rebuilt with a folding roof. Those without

the money to have this done will simply chop off the roofs of their cars, and leave it at that. With few rainy days to worry about, such a car may actually pass as a convertible.

Sunroofs are the next best thing. They offer certain advantages—security, easier maintenance—and there are dozens of companies which do nothing but install sunroofs. The best sunroof for sun lovers is the ragtop variety, which opens up the largest chunk of roof, but it is noisy at highway speeds, and is best suited for cruising around town, with a blond beach girl sticking her head out of it.

The pop-up or pop-out hard sunroofs are smaller but stronger, and best if you don't want your Blaupunkt yanked.

(Translation: if you don't want your expensive status tape-deck-stereo radio stolen from your dashboard.)

The glass moonroof is a possibility, although it can heat up the car unpleasantly on hot, sunny days if left shut in the parking lot. If you buy one, it should either have a panel to shut out the light, or should be designed to open just a crack to let out heat without allowing access to your car from outside. (It should be fully openable from inside, of course, or else it's a pretty wimpy excuse for a sunroof.)

Fake convertible tops— vinyl roofs with dummy ribs built in—are too ridiculous to even talk about.

Accessory to the Chrome

Okay. So you know you will be judged by what car you drive. You know you will do a lot of your living in your car. You know you will come to think of your car as part of your family. It's time, then, to think seriously about really putting your mark on the car; imbuing it with your personality. The best way to do this—the way traditional to Southern California—is to *accessorize* it. You must *self-actualize* your car, perhaps even before you self-actualize yourself. Here are some of the most popular personality traits which you can buy for your car at the dealer or accessory shop.

THE CAR BRA

Arguably the kinkiest item of lingerie ever, this "bra" is made of black leatherette thick enough to deflect sharp rocks and is big enough to fit the front end of your car. It is intended to protect the front end from dings, dents, and abrasions from gravel, sand, insects, slow-moving pedestrians—but mostly its high-tech look is intended to proclaim, "Beneath this bra is a car *really worth protecting*. An *expensive* car."

Like vinyl living-room

furniture covers or curlers worn in public, the car bra (which looks like nothing so much as a giant muzzle) tends to detract from as much as enhance appearance; for this reason it is suggested that the car bra be used only *after* the car has suffered front-end defacement. At this point the bra is functionally useless, of course, which qualifies it for the highest echelon of status symbols.

THE MERCEDES ROOF HOIST

At various times we have all been faced with the nagging problem of wanting to remove the heavy, detachable hard-top roofs from our Mercedes 380SL's (or 450's, or 350's, et cetera) when there hasn't been an extra pair of hands around to help with this cumbersome chore.

Well, ever resourceful in a crisis, Californians have come up with a neat solution: the SL Top Hoist, a hundred-dollar configuration of clamps, pulleys, and cable which attaches to the ceiling of your garage and allows you to lift the Mercedes's roof all by yourself.

Please remember to install yours where it will not interfere with your automatic garage-door opener.

THE RAINBOW DECAL

There are in Southern California (and especially in spots like Topanga) a faithful few who have never forgotten the golden age of the late 1960s. Most of these chosen people are scattered far and wide now, but they proudly carry an emblem affixed to the rear windows of their cars. It is the transparent rainbow decal, and the next time you see it on that beat-up old VW bus going ten miles per hour in

front of you, don't be impatient. Sit back, relax, and smile, secure in the knowledge that although you may get there late, you are being bathed in the most positive of vibrations and the best of karma.

THE CAR COVER

The covered wagon, which brought early settlers to California, lives on in the cloth car cover. An absolute must for any car parked regularly in the sun (which destroys the car's finish) or in the shade (where strafing by birds occurs).

The newcomer to Southern California might mistakenly assume that the car cover is meant to keep rain off the car. No way. Rain is always welcome to a parked car, since it washes off the ambient filth that collects faster here than anywhere else. (Rain is, however, a real problem for moving cars. Unused to wet weather, Southern Californians on the freeways respond to a heavy downpour by driving faster, in order to get safely out of the rain sooner, and by tailgating, the better to see clearly the cars ahead of them.)

The first thing to do when you buy your car cover (preferably one specifically tailored to your model) is to stencil your license-plate number on it in figures about a foot high. Then, consider replacing your antenna with one that retracts automatically, to make the process of covering up smoother.

Now, take your car cover with you when you go on a date, and use it for the one purpose to which it is really best suited. Drape it over your car, lift the edge, crawl back in with your date, and *voilà:* a giant hanky to cover your panky.

WINDOW TINTING

Why would anyone who's not ashamed of what he's doing want all the windows of his car darkened to a near-black opacity? Presumably the very popular tinted window (businesses exist which do nothing but tint) is meant to ward off the hot Southern California sun, but there is a far more personal motivation than that.

Tinted windows not only keep you cool, they keep you Cool. Too Cool to be seen. So Cool that I can see you but you can't see me. With this automotive equivalent of dark sunglasses, everyone can avoid the prying eyes of fans, real or imagined. Anyone can be a star in his own car.

Especially popular on BMWs and Saab Turbos.

SHEEPSKIN SEAT COVERS

Perhaps you don't think you need these.

Perhaps you think real fur upholstery in a car is a bit gaudy. Just wait.

Just wait until you've parked your car at Zuma Beach for six hours on a hot, sunny Saturday in August and you come back in your swimsuit and sunburn and sit down on all that black vinyl upholstery.

After you get out of the hospital you'll be ready to kill defenseless sheep for a set of these. It's not necessary, however. Sheepskin seat covers are available in hundreds of different styles all over Southern California.

The correct ones to have, cover the *whole* of each front seat, without a lot of messy straps behind the seat backs. And please—none of that synthetic sheepskin. If you can't afford the real thing, use the poor man's (or surfer's) sheepskin: a large terrycloth Budweiser beach towel.

Advertising claims are made that sheepskin also keeps you warm in cold weather. In Southern California, however, it is not possible to prove this conclusively.

ΣLP Yourself

The basic idea of the vanity plate (officially an "ELP," or Environmental License Plate, since proceeds for their sales go to an environmental fund, affording the perfect excuse for vanity) is to personalize your car, and probably the most popular plates are those bannering the owner's name, or nickname:

TAMMI

The next wrinkle is name plus possessiveness:

STEVES

(Occasionally the apostrophe will be painted in by the owner.)

Next comes the gift-car plate:

4 JENNI

And special interest plates:

10S NE1 (immediately imitated by TENSNE1)

Sexual advertising is not uncommon:

R U E Z

HOTNBED

FOXY GUY

Nor is wishful thinking

OH4AJAG

Professional pride is often evident:

C ME 2 SU

UROLOGY

occasionally becoming absurd:

HOT CPA

D AND C

Tailgaters are discouraged by:

TOOHI2C

while people being tailgated may be startled to read this plate in their rearview mirror:

TIH2

But the most Californian plate of all is probably the Redundancy Plate, which reads

380SL

on a Mercedes 380SL,

XJ JAG

on a Jaguar XJ, and so forth.

29

Valet Parking

Do not fool yourself into thinking that valet parking is primarily a *convenience.* After all, finding a parking space is not much of a problem in most of Southern California. And it rarely saves time, since it usually takes the valet just as much time to get your car as it would take you.

No, valet parking exists for its own sake. It is a status symbol, and a way of life. In fact, one of the signs of making it in Southern California is that you find yourself buying a snap-apart key ring because you are encountering so many valets.

Valet parking is not merely chic at restaurants and businesses; it is also de rigueur at any party in Beverly Hills, Bel-Air, and such. This allows you to make the same grand entrance at your friends' houses that you make at restaurants. You can pull right up to the door and show everyone your car.

And who are the valets? Your basic status valet is a young, good-looking surfer type. It is important to hotels and restaurants to give guests a good first impression—after all, the valet is the first person to greet you—and most such establishments prefer this image of radiant Californianism. Many places like to use novelty valets: only women, only bodybuilders, only French-speaking.

The biggest concern most people have about valet parking is what to tip. Despite what a valet may tell you, the base tip is one dollar. Of course in Southern California, where tipping big is considered an act of self-improvement, you should always be watching for opportunities to tip more. Here, then, is a list of special circumstances, each of which may earn the attendant an extra fifty cents to one dollar.

1. You slip and fall or otherwise exit car ungracefully and attendant does not laugh.

2. Attendant remembers your name.
3. Attendant remembers your car.
4. Attendant does not change the station, move the seat, smoke in, or soil your car. (Usually you can't tell this until after you have exchanged your tip for your keys.)
5. Attendant compliments you on your car.
6. Attendant asks for your autograph even though you are not a celebrity.
7. Attendant *does not* ask for your autograph even though you are a celebrity.
8. You used to be a parking attendant.

If the attendant strips your gears, crashes your car, damages the finish, or steals something, you should *never* tip more than one dollar.

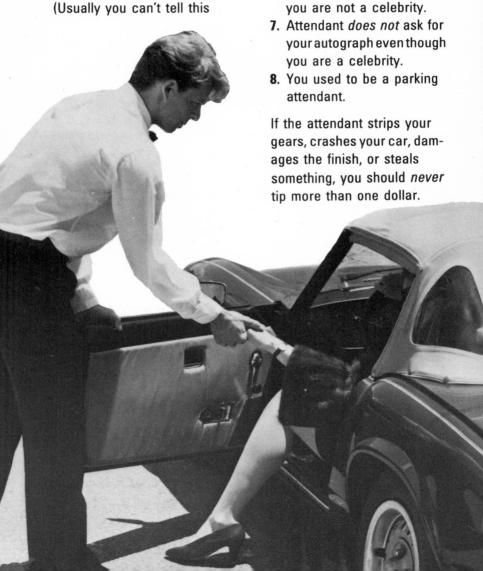

RULES OF THE ROAD

The following rules are supplementary to rules in the California Vehicle Code, and as such it should not be construed that they are legally binding. They are, however, *socially* binding. That is, they are the principles commonly accepted by all true Southern California drivers. Failure to understand these rules may result in loss of cool, loss of friends, or loss of tan. Reinstatement of any of these is frequently difficult, and it is therefore suggested that you study them carefully now in order to avoid embarrassment later.

MINORS

All children of legal elementary-school age must be able to discourse knowledgeably upon the subject of the relative merits of their parents' or siblings' cars, as well as the prices of those cars, and whether they are leased, paid for, or financed.

NO LICENSE PLATES

All licensed California drivers must be prepared to drive for many weeks (sometimes months) without license plates upon their vehicles, while proper plates are being prepared. During this time they must display, in the space normally allotted to license plates, an advertising placard for the dealership where the car was purchased, however embarrassing that dealer's locale or slogan may be. During this period it is expected that the driver will not attempt to take unfair advantage of the car's anonymity, since if the police want to nail you, they will anyway.

DRIVE-UP WINDOWS

Your examination for a driver's license may include a simple test of your ability to negotiate the drive-up window at a bank, dry cleaner, or fast-food establishment. The examiner will judge you on your ability to read the menu quickly if there are people in line behind your car, to speak clearly into the microphone when placing your order even if that microphone is in the form of a clown's face, and to approach the pickup window without endangering your side mirror.

You will be denied a driver's license if you (a) forget part of your order *after* passing the order microphone, or (b) drop any of your food or money between your car window and the pickup window, or (c) fail to accurately count your money while driving to or from the restaurant, or (d) fail to ask for extra napkins.

TIRE CHEWERS

This picture shows a row of steel shark's teeth embedded in the pavement to prevent cars from crossing, usually into or out of parking lots, without shredding their tires. The teeth deflect in one direction, permitting one-way passage, but sadistic planners have learned to mount these on hills, often right next to a necessary stop (such as to take a parking check). Thus a car that passes safely across these teeth, then stops, can still roll back a few inches and be creamed. Drivers of

manual-transmission cars are advised to dive-bomb such obstacles.

Occasionally the warning signs get turned around and point in the wrong direction. Good luck.

DATING

If you are operating a motor vehicle carrying a passenger of the opposite sex with whom you have not previously consorted (a "first date"), you must inform that passenger that you are merely driving your brother's Pinto while your Rolls is in the shop. Failure to so inform the passenger may result in the revocation of your opportunity for a second date.

PASSENGERS IN PICKUPS

Passengers riding in the back of pickup trucks must ordinarily be seated in folding lawn chairs. They should display a can of beer and should smile, regardless of how terrified or uncomfortable they may be.

DEPRESSION

Since bad moods are counterproductive to safe driving (the *California Driver's Handbook* advises you to "maintain a smiling attitude"), all Southern Californians should be alert to signs of depression. Most people have found that when they are depressed a trip to the Pep Boys store for an accessory for the car is a successful antidote.

ACKNOWLEDGMENTS

If another driver shall permit you to pass him, or to turn before he does at an intersection, or shall otherwise yield his way to you, you must acknowledge him by smiling and waving. Failure to do so may result in your being thought weird, foreign, or unmellow.

FLASHING

At all hours of day or night, regardless of light conditions, owners of Porsche automobiles must flash their headlights when approaching other Porsche automobiles going in the opposite direction (toward them), as a greeting and an acknowledgment of the other driver's good taste and judgment.

THOMAS BROTHERS MAPS

Each driver in the Los Angeles area must have a copy of this map in the car at all times because the region is unbelievably difficult to negotiate otherwise. Drivers are advised to practice reading this map before driving. It is just like any ordinary road map except that it has hundreds of pages and any single route requires cross-references to at least half a dozen different pages. A safe driver is one who can read the map without slowing down, which could seriously inconvenience other drivers.

TICKETS

Traffic tickets come in threes. If you receive one, you may expect two more within a few months. If you are stopped and ticketed by a single law enforcement officer, remain calm and confident. You may be able to talk your way out of the ticket in traffic court. If there are two officers, forget it. You haven't got a prayer in court. The best way to avoid tickets is to avoid detection by police, and the best way to avoid police is to avoid Winchell's Donut Houses.

STREET NAMES AND ROUTES

Street names change without warning in Southern California, and any one neighborhood has the same street names repeated with small changes (Jones Road, Jones Street, Jones Court, Jones Boulevard) on many completely separate roads all within a small area. Furthermore, any one street may appear to end abruptly at a cross street, only to begin again some distance away. For this reason written and oral directions may appear complicated, but they should be heeded carefully. Experienced Southern California drivers always allow an extra twenty to thirty percent travel time for the time that they will spend completely lost within a few hundred yards of their destination.

35

BOTTS DOTS

It being the inalienable franchise of all drivers to fall asleep, catnap, or otherwise fade while driving on the freeway, it is also the privilege of that freeway to awaken the driver. For this purpose, Southern California's freeways are equipped with Botts Dots: round white bumps punctuating the broken lines between lanes. When the tires of a wandering car drift over these bumps, a thumping is transmitted through the body of the car to awaken the driver.

Regular early-morning commuters trust Botts Dots more than Westclox to leave them alert for work.

PEDESTRIANS

The following two (2) rules exist simultaneously:

Rule number one: Jaywalkers are treated with great severity.

Rule number two: Jaywalkers are treated with great deference.

Pedestrians are, after all, a *novelty* in Southern California, and neither they nor drivers have quite got the hang of it yet. Thus, sooner or later, *everyone* gets a jaywalking ticket (Rule number one).

At the same time, pedestrians *always* have the right of way. Failure to screech to a stop when so much as one foot is in the road will earn a driver a ticket (Rule number two).

Ten Things People Do in Cars While Waiting at the Light

1. Check out drivers to the right and left.

2. Make date with someone in the next car.

3. Apply mascara. (Datsun 280ZX especially.)

4. Practice the drums on top of steering wheel.

5. Lower convertible top.

6. Pick nose.

7. Sing.

8. Read page forty-one of the Thomas Brothers map.

9. Wipe outside of windshield from driver's seat by reaching around through window with napkin from Bob's Big Boy, causing foot to slip off brake, car to move forward, and pedestrian to break into a trot.

10. Talk on telephone.

Week 2
FASHION

The key to Southern Californian fashion is one word. Casual.

Here, the ultimate fashion error is to overdress. An easy mistake to avoid, you might think, until you consider that "overdressed" may mean wearing a T-shirt tucked in, instead of loose. "Overdressed" in certain circumstances may be when your sweat shirt and sweat pants are the same color. And sporting a necktie nearly always results in being judged "overdressed."

There are exceptions, of course. You will need a tuxedo or evening gown when attending the Academy Award presentations. The right fur gets you snappier service on Rodeo Drive. But otherwise, casual.

Or, to put it more casually, cazh.

Cazh is wearing athletic clothing to a business meeting, a sweat suit to a dinner date, surf trunks to school.

Cazh is having the right shoes for every occasion, and they're all sneakers.

Cazh is when you own more blue jeans than cuff links, more running shorts than collar stays, and more T-shirts than everything else put together.

This week you will learn how to loosen your collar (by about four buttons), to kick off your socks (a neat trick, come to think of it), and to go fully cazh.

Everyday Wear

Ideally you will own two wardrobes of athletic gear: one for athletics, the other for every other waking moment. The wardrobes may be identical; only their odor distinguishes them.

The reason that Southern Californians always appear to be just coming from or going to a workout is that that is exactly what they are doing. But if you are constitutionally or morally unsuited for strenuous activity, you can still look as though you at least *approve* of the idea by sporting sporting garb.

Sneakers

You will own sneakers for all occasions, but the most *California* sneakers under your bed will be Vans slip-ons (center foreground), which are made and sold in Southern California. High status is also conferred on Nike, Puma, New Balance, and especially K-Swiss (to the right of the Vans); lower status for Adidas and off-brands. For fashionable occa-

sions, all-leather sneakers and any with Velcro closures are recommended. The Puma Davis Cup, for instance (center rear), may be worn with a tuxedo.

Thongs

As soon as possible you will want to see how many days you can go without wearing shoes, only thongs. Thongs, also called flip-flops and go-aheads (because you can't go backward in them), range in price from sixteen-dollar brand-name surf-shop models down to the eighty-nine-cent all-rubber discount-store variety. The latter is the cooler. There is a seventy-nine-cent rubber-with-plastic-straps thong, but it hurts. In any case, you should start building up good thong calluses now. Incidentally, the coolest footwear of all is no footwear.

Sweats

There are two ways to go here: designer or generic.

The problem is complicated by the fact that generic sweats, from the army-navy store or the jeans store, come in more designer colors than the signed designer sweats. (Henceforth you will say "sweats" to refer to sweat shirts, sweat pants, and related items.)

The solution depends upon

where you live. If you are in an upscale, Beverly Hills–type community, you had better stick to sweats with the Puma, Nike, Fila, or Camp Beverly Hills logo. In the more pretentious parts of the Valley, the same applies. In other parts of the Valley, insignia like Pierre Cardin are proper. Elsewhere—especially if you are under forty, in school, or belong to a *serious* gym— stick to the plain, old-fashioned Brand X sweats. Your choice of fancy colors will diminish as your athletic prowess increases.

Yes, you may cut the sleeves off your sweat shirt, or turn it inside out, or both. Do not follow suit with sweat pants.

Where can you wear sweats? Studio meetings (if you are a writer, and thus allowed to look funky, it makes them think you are more creative). Shopping. Most restaurants. Funerals. Do not wear sweats to traffic court.

The Nylon Wallet

The correct wallet is made of heavy nylon fabric, frequently with a sunset-and-palms motif screened on one side. It has a loop for your keys, and it is washable. This wallet is perfect for carrying everything when your are in athletic gear (which is most of the time) and have no pockets. The wallet is closed with Velcro; it makes a distinctive sound when it is opened,

which, in Southern California, happens a lot.

The Day of the Dolfin

These Dolfins (*sic*) migrate all the way from Shillington, Pennsylvania, where they come into the world, to Southern California, where they turn up all along the beaches and as far inland as Jane Fonda's Workout in Beverly Hills. They are the nylon athletic shorts with the distinctive half-inch vertical stripes (colors alternating with white) which are the most important and correct brand to own. Quite simply, they have the best cut and the sturdiest material; not incidentally, they also have the Dolfin name in cursive clearly visible. Dolfins are also available in solid colors and with different-colored panels. All are correct. For the true California Girl look, wear the all-white Dolfins, one size too small. With that one exception, Dolfins are appropriate for both sexes.

OPs

OPs (pronounced as two separate letters) refers to a whole line of clothes that grew out of surfing styles, but the expression "OPs" tends to mean specifically OP shorts. OPs are cut similarly to jeans, but with elastic-back waistbands, no belt loops, and the front pockets stitched onto

the outside. The classic OP is made of corduroy (narrow or wide wale), but the shorts also come in plain cotton. All have the OP insignia embroidered onto a front pocket.

OPs are the classic, basic, all-purpose, wear-them-everywhere shorts; the shorts equivalent of Levi's. (By the way, cutoff Levi's are rare in Southern California and are not fashionable; save them for car-washing.) The competing brands of shorts, like Grapevines and Pacific Coast Highway, are sometimes acceptable, too. So are OP-style long pants.

OPs are part of the official uniform of beach policemen.

Odd Closures

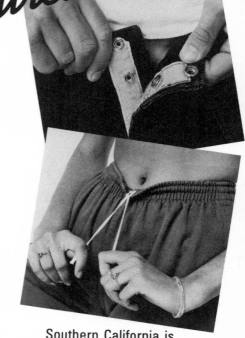

Californians rarely require that their clothes protect them from the elements, and perhaps because of this they tend to experiment with unusual forms of closure on their apparel.

Drawstrings are a standard way of securing waistbands on pants and shorts; so is *elastic*. Many pants have both. *Zippers* are generally unpopular. Southern Californians far prefer a fly sealed by *Velcro* (so much fun to pull open) or, in the case of the ubiquitous Levi's 501's, buttons. Velcro turns up on shoes, wallets, watchbands, and more.

Southern California is also the birthplace of *wrap shorts* for women—an incredibly complicated apparatus for achieving a casual look.

The T-Shirt Collection

HUSSONG'S CANTINA, ENSENADA

As soon as you finish reading this, you should start work on your printed T-shirt collection. Building one takes a long time, much love and patience, and no self-respecting Southern Californian is without an extensive assortment which, owing to the benevolent weather, is on permanent, revolving display.

These are special because they involved a trip into Mexico; a trip during which you and everyone with you got exceptionally drunk.

The highlights of the average T-shirt collection are those shirts which, out of everyone you know, only you own. They may relate to a remote travel destination, an obscure bar, a special concert. They may relate to a place where you live, spend a lot of time, or would like to spend a lot of time.

And there are classic T-shirts—old masters, really—which belong in every collection. They are:

GOLD'S GYM

From the bodybuilding capital of the world, Venice Beach.

HEAVEN

It may be a bit of a letdown to learn that Heaven is a boutique in Century City, but these T-shirts are a staple among the bicoastal set.

SEX WAX

It's a surfboard wax, if you must know. Surfers' T-shirts are available—and desirable—in long-sleeved versions.

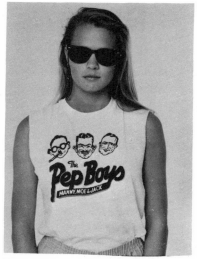

THE PEP BOYS: MANNY, MOE, AND JACK

From the Pep Boys chain of auto supply stores; notable because the shirts are exceptionally cheap.

ANY T-SHIRT FROM HAWAII

But particularly a long-sleeved T-shirt from a surfing supply business.

Note: T-shirts are generally worn not tucked in. But if your T-shirt is too long (like minidress length) you should cut it off to taste. Unless you are wearing it as a minidress.

Aloha Shirts

Very chic because they come from Hawaii, which is the only place a Southern Californian considers hipper than Southern California. Older aloha shirts are especially prized, and fetch a high price in used clothing boutiques. Do not tuck in an aloha shirt. No, the top button is not missing—they're made that way.

The Hooded Mexican Pullover

A Southern California classic. All cotton and musty-smelling. Traditional among surfers. Ideally, you should buy yours on a jaunt to Tijuana. The colors are about as fast as a California lawn snail, but fortunately you will be able to buy a new pullover for less than it would cost even to think about washing it.

Levi's

Every year, in late August, a war is waged throughout Southern California. The spoils of that war are known only by a cryptic number: 501's. But every Southern California child, every college student, in fact nearly everyone under forty, knows what 501's are. And nearly every one of them owns at least one and probably several of them. In some circles, the more decrepit the 501's, the more they are prized.

The war is a price war waged by clothing stores for the back-to-school season. 501's are the original shrink-to-fit button-fly indigo blue heavyweight denim, all-cotton Levi's jeans. For your true Southern Californian, no other jean will do.

There are two ways for 501's to look. Crisp and new, in deep, dark blue; ideal for more formal occasions, with a jacket and tie, or for date night at the movies in Westwood. Or incredibly faded, with at least one knee worn clean through. This look is the result of constant wear and constant, brutal washings. The former look can be maintained by washing in cold water but more generally it is the result of buying a fresh pair whenever the darkest pair you have starts to fade.

It is undesirable to wear 501's at any intermediate stage of fading. What you do between crisp and ragged is your own problem.

Western Drag

You can't get much farther west than California, except maybe Texas.

And California maintains a large cult of cowboys. These are not the "urban cowboys" who dress up in western gear only on weekends—these are full-time cowboys who wear boots, Stetson hats, western shirts, and bolo ties every day because it is appropriate to their jobs; jobs as computer programmers, lawyers, and car salesmen.

So the horses they ride now are under the hoods of four-by-four pickup trucks; so the frontier is the far western edge of the San Fernando Valley: it doesn't matter. As long as there are lizards and ostriches there will be four-hundred-dollar Lucchese boots from Jonathan Western in Redondo Beach. As long as there is eighteen-karat gold there will be spurs and collar tips. The cowboys haven't died out. They have moved to the Palomino Club—the Gilley's of North Hollywood.

Chains of Gold

This look is largely out of favor, now, except in certain time-warped sections of the Valley, and wherever Sammy Davis, Jr., is performing. Once the hallmark of the record-industry types, it is now considered an embarrassing cliché. Even in California.

The "Whore" Look

What would you call a woman in a low-cut tube top showing most of the upper portion of the breasts, tight short-shorts showing most of the lower portion of the cheeks, and high platform shoes? Don't answer too quickly. In Southern California it's a perfectly normal look. You just might call her "Mom."

Weather Confusion

Within the narrow range of temperatures and weather conditions found in most of Southern California, residents are exceptionally sensitive to marginal differences. But, since different people have different thresholds, this scene is not uncommon in the Southland, especially in the spring and fall.

49

All-White Outfits

In the rest of America, all-white outfits are reserved for satiric writers (Mark Twain, Tom Wolfe), nurses, Good Humor men, and the sister who hasn't come downstairs in seventeen years.

But in California, all-white is a distinctive, idiosyncratic look. It speaks of a sunny disposition, of an airy coolness in hot weather, and most important, *it makes your tan look really great.*

The look is shared by men and women, and is generally composed of cool cotton, linen, or silk. It is hell to keep clean.

Week 3

BODS

Perhaps you were dreading this part. Perhaps you thought, "My body could never be up to Southern California standards. One look at me and they'll know."

Stop worrying.

While it is certainly of tremendous importance that you have the best possible body, it is far more important that you have the right attitude about bods in general. It is the karma of body culture that matters. The mind is a powerful tool, even in Southern California, and enough positive thinking can project an illusion of health. And if that fails for any reason, all you have to do is surround yourself with enough athletic clothing, exercise equipment, and rooms full of fit people working out, and no one will ever notice your body.

A Visit to the Health Club

First of all, you *will* join a health club or, at the very least, an aerobics or dance studio. This can be a daunting move for the timid, because your introductory tour will be conducted by a Brad or Melissa who is physically perfect and smiles a lot, and who behaves like the offspring of a camp counselor and an aluminum siding salesman.

Brad or Melissa—or both—will ask you some simple questions, and you don't want to hem and haw in answering. How many times a week do you play racquetball? Four? Five? Eleven? Are you an expert? Would you like to be put on the competition roster right now?

You will be shown an aerobics class that is just starting. Don't let the energy level get you down. Ask to see an aerobics class that is just ending. This instructor tells you that her name is Melissa, too, though her body is telling you "Victoria Principal." It appears that aerobics Melissa is on speed, but Brad and Melissa anticipate your question and set you straight. Aerobics Melissa eats nothing but bread for three days, then nothing but protein for three days, then three days of leafy greens, three of spring water, and three of fasting to *purify her body.* Don't scoff. Within a week of joining her aerobics class, you'll be up to leafy greens yourself.

At the running track note whether a Walkman is in or out at this particular club. A mistake in this department could lead to ridicule. At the pool, note the ratio of lap swimmers to tanners; one to ten is about normal. A wider ratio may indicate that the club is too frivolous; a narrower ratio, too earnest. In the Jacuzzi you will notice four people negotiating what looks like either a drug or a movie deal. It is, in fact, both.

In the locker room the fact that you will actually have to disrobe in front of people who are in much better shape than you will finally occur to you. Don't bother to ask—there's no reduced fee for changing at home.

Finally, the snack bar/lounge, where the Beautiful and the Tanned are enjoying salads of sunflower seeds, shredded carrots, and sprouts, washed down by big frosty mugs of beer. *Pay very close attention here.* Note the singles scene here.

Ultimately, it is the reason you are joining the club in the first place. If they're not the sort of people you'd want to hit on (or be hit on by) in a singles bar, they're not the sort of people you'd want to work out with.

Upon returning to the membership office, Brad and Melissa will confide that today is the last day of an employees' incentive program that allows them to offer you a twelve-year membership at an unprecedented low rate.

Take it.

Bodybuilding

Southern California is also the bodybuilding capital of America, if not the world. In particular, in Venice, where iron is vigorously pumped right on the beach for the benefit of spectators.

This conspicuous body-culture results in a heightened awareness of technical knowledge about the body for everyone in the state. In

California no one will never complain of a strained arm or a sore back. Instead he will say, knowingly, "Boy, I really pulled that triceps outta shape yesterday," or, "Wow, are my lats killing me!"

No Fat Chicks

A phrase thought endlessly amusing, especially by surfers and high-school stoners, "No Fat Chicks" generally appears on bumper stickers or license-plate frames. It certainly says something about Southern California values, just as its variations—a silhouette of a fat woman with a superimposed international NO symbol; the phrase "Save a whale: harpoon a fat chick" —say something about Southern California humor. To say that it is cruel, elitist, and sexist is not in the Southern California spirit. After all, we're talking about fat chicks.

The Battle of the Network Stars

Watch these TV specials whenever possible and observe very, very closely. Because far more than the 1984 Olympics, the Network Battles show the true state of California athletic aspirations.

True, not everyone in the Southland participates in the Baseball Dunk or the Soap Stars Tug of War, but the spirit of the shows is right on the mark. Notice that the players always smile. Notice that when they lose, they laugh. Notice how Morgan Fairchild and Tom Selleck look in bathing suits.

Remember, it's not whether you win or lose that counts, it's how fantastic you look doing it.

Vitamins

Two questions you might as well get used to right now are

    A. What vitamins do you do?

and

    B. Say, do you have any Vitamin B in the house?

    Your own individually tailored selection of vitamins is very special, very personal—rather like your mantra. But unlike the case with your mantra, you should be prepared to describe it in detail. Have some stirring before-and-after experiences to describe. Other Southern Californians are *always* interested in hearing of new benefits derived from vitamins (or plankton or garlic injections or whatever). Make someone's day. Tell him that twenty onion tablets a day seem to have reduced the likelihood of

contracting herpes.

Get yourself a little compartmentalized plastic vitamin case. Take it out in the middle of some activity—a board meeting is ideal—stop everything, sort out your selection very carefully, then swallow the largest possible variety of pill sizes, shapes, and colors, one at a time. If you are dealing with other Californians, they will discover a newfound respect for you.

Drugs

This is not to advocate drug abuse but simply to explain that if drugs *are* a big part of your life it is entirely possible to integrate them into your new California ways. Here's how.

1. If you are a studio executive, *never* forget to leave a pass at the gate to admit your dealer to the studio lot.

2. Only buy domestic (that is, California) marijuana. The kinds grown up in Humboldt County are the best in the country (on the mainland, at least) and they provide employment to hardworking Americans. For the same reason, Hawaiian is acceptable as a special-occasion delicacy.

3. Treat your dealer as though he were one of the family. After all, if you cheat him, he may turn around and cheat your own kid, or mother.

4. If you are in the public eye, you must denounce drug abuse publicly, but do not confuse this with cutting it out of your private life.

5. It is perfectly acceptable to cut coffee and tea out of your life on the grounds that they are harmful drugs *without* easing back on the controlled substances.

6. Never act surprised when someone asks, "What drugs do you use for work?"

7. It isn't nice to hog the bathroom at parties, but it's sure fashionable.

Aging

(SILVER THREADS AMONG THE GOLD, OR, AGING IS WHEN THE ROOTS OF YOUR BLOND HAIR TURN FROM BLACK TO WHITE)

Some of you may be planning to become old one day and are perhaps wondering, "How can I possibly fit age into my new Southern California lifestyle? I thought nobody in California was old."

Don't worry. Plenty of people in California are well over thirty-nine years old, especially since the repeal of the Maximum Age Statute (the so-called "Benny Law"). But there *is* an art to growing old California-style that is unlike aging anywhere else.

First, it is considered poor form to look your age. There are four main detours around this problem—Exercise, Cosmetics, Wardrobe, and Surgery—any of which are acceptable, though the whole package is the most popular route. Further, it is a source of great pride to surprise people by telling them your actual age, and it is the customary response to say,

"Gee, you sure don't look it."

The most daring but also the most successful solution is to lie by claiming to be *older* than you actually are. Thus, if you are, say, twenty-eight, you might claim to be thirty-seven, or forty-one, impressing even the most jaded cynic with your remarkably youthful appearance.

Second, the ordinary signs of advancing years are not necessarily indications of geriatric decline. Californians customarily have children when in their late teens, making under-forty grandparents commonplace. And perpetual exposure to the sun may create an *illusion* of advancing age in the form of wrinkles (or, as they are called in Southern California, character lines).

Third, California is not noted for mathematical skills, and Southern Californians may be excused for losing track of numbers in the high forties and fifties.

So you may rest assured that while the little old lady from Pasadena has probably moved to a condo in La Jolla or Santa Barbara, she *is* alive and well and doing aerobics right there next to you in the magenta leotard.

Nip and Tuck

HAIR TRANSPLANT
EYE JOB
NOSE JOB
CHIN JOB
FACE LIFT
CHEMICAL PEEL
DERMABRASION

CALIFORNIA SCARS

1. SURF KNOBS—from rubbing against surfboards too long

2. SPRINKLER SCARS—sooner or later everyone trips over a built-in sprinkler on the lawn

3. LIFT AND TUCK SCARS—the price of maintenance

4. ACUPUNCTURE SCARS—usually a relic of the Nixon era, they are generally invisible

5. CAR SORES—like bed sores, except that you spend only one third of your life in bed

DEATH TAKES A FUNERAL

> *"I can't come in to work this afternoon—I have to take a funeral."* —*overheard in The Industry*

Like rain, clean air, and bad moods, death is one of those believe-it-or-not rarities that, nevertheless, do occasionally occur in Southern California, and you should be prepared for it.

There are two kinds of death—regular and celebrity. Regular deaths are an embarrassment in the Southland and will not be discussed in any depth, because they are boring. Celebrity deaths are the fun kind.

A good celebrity death must be planned carefully, for maximum publicity value. If it is to be of the scandalous variety, not too much information should be given out at any one time. Instead, a false lead must be released at first. This is invariably a report of

death "by natural causes." Immediately you must start the rumors in The Industry. Within a few days one or two of these rumors will be allowed to solidify into fact, which may then be reported to the press. Next, an inquest should be either demanded or resisted by the family or friends of the deceased. In either case the inquest itself must become a media event, with new facts and specula- tions being released on a regular schedule. Finally the results of the chemical tests are sent to the *National Enquirer.*

At last the deceased may be disposed of, either by burial at Forest Lawn or, in the popular new fashion, by crema- tion and distribution of ashes at sea, which is very nice because it includes a boat ride.

After this point the dead

59

remain useful, even if the celebrity death was of the nonscandalous variety. There are the ex post facto lunch appointments to be made (it is customary in The Industry to announce that you were due to have lunch with the deceased the week after he or she died). The deceased is added to the guidebooks and tours of the Stars' Death Spots.

Next come tributes—on newsmagazine TV shows, in the press, at the revival movie houses—in which it is discovered that the late celebrity was always loved and admired by all the people who hadn't given him or her a job in years, but who can now recall—verbatim—lengthy compliments paid to themselves decades earlier by the deceased, whose credibility as the grand old man or lady of The Industry is suddenly a foregone conclusion.

And finally the deceased goes into the real estate business. With so few celebrities actually born in Southern California, it is customary for real estate agents to boast of a property being the *deathplace* of someone famous; and in any case with the celebrity conveniently unavailable for comment, the number of homes (especially apartments) said to have once been occupied by that person is allowed, by law, to grow geometrically.

FOREST LAWN MEMORIAL PARK is something like Disneyland, only instead of cartoon characters it is all about dead people. Thus, Southern Californians are regularly buried in a park that also contains the world's largest religious painting (195′ × 45′), a full-size replica of Leonardo's *The Last Supper*, just like the original only in stained glass, and reproductions of many famous historical buildings and most of the major sculptures (again life size) of Michelangelo, including the famous statue of David, gazing as he has since time immemorial out across the rooftops of Glendale. It is not proper to snicker; Forest Lawn is very, very serious.

This is without a doubt the place to be, if you're dead.

The Nine Rules of Tennis in Southern California

1. Tennis clothes by Fila are required. They are the most expensive. Always arrive on the court in a Fila warmup suit, regardless of the weather.

2. Movie stars win in a manner proportionate to how much they earn. No star with an income over one million dollars loses. Clint Eastwood wins, always.

3. Studio heads always win.

4. There are "A" courts and games, and "B" courts and games. A player of "A" ability may play a player of "B" ability, provided that the "B" player represents an "A" level of money or power.

5. Open a new can of balls at least every set.

6. Your tennis court must run north/south, or no one will play at your house because the sun might get in his eyes.

7. Always include an elaborate lunch and a screening with any tennis game you host.

8. You must have a refrigerator by your court and a telephone. A phone at each end is a thoughtful touch.

9. The term "good shot" refers to a studio executive hitting one over the net.

Sports

Certain sports are more Southern Californian than others. Familiarize yourself with them. That means at least knowing the fundamentals, even if you can't actually perform them where you live. It's not impossible—think of how in the early-1960s heyday of surf movies, everyone in Kansas knew all about "hanging ten." Here are today's California sports with tips on how to adapt them for where you live.

BEACH VOLLEYBALL

Just like volleyball you play anywhere else, but you empty about a cup and a half of sand into your shorts while playing. Generally undertaken only for fun, tournaments can draw large crowds to the nets, which are set up all along the California beaches.

SKATEBOARDING

This, of course, is done everywhere, but it has a special meaning in Southern California's car culture, where the skateboard is the general mode of transportation for the under-sixteen set. A fifteen-year-old without a skateboard is like a seventeen-year-old without a car. Ultimately, it is necessary to learn how to ride a skateboard through traffic while holding a full-sized surfboard under one arm. When you're really adept at controlled weaving, go out and frighten motorists.

Skateboarders have developed a popular myth among themselves that they are a special breed of rebels, dedicated to a life far removed from the snares of parental authority. This is especially prevalent among the more radical (or "rad") skateboarders, who specialize in dramatic, trick maneuvers, often involving ramps, drainage ducts, and other accoutrements of the skate-park. If you aspire to join their ranks, try to develop a contempt for non-skateboarders.

BMX AND BEACH CRUISER BICYCLING

Beach Cruisers are the somewhat old-fashioned-looking fat-tired one-speed coaster-brake bikes favored by surfers and beach kinds in general. They are sufficiently heavy-duty to allow them to be ridden up across curbs, over some sandy areas, and in and out among pedestrians at high speeds. Learn to do wheelies on these. BMX bikes are the kind that look like a heavy-duty child's bike, with small wheels. Ideally these should be very expensively outfitted with custom alloy parts and racing accessories for riding off-road. Fitting out your kid's bike is to today's Southern California father what buying your kid an expensive train set used to be elsewhere—a guilt-free way of spoiling the little kid in yourself. And, as with trains, adults tend to look somewhat foolish playing with these bikes.

ROLLER SKATING

Of course this is popular everywhere, but there are a few indications that it means something more in California. Signs that say NO ROLLER SKATING IN THE BANK, PLEASE. Moving violation tickets issued for roller skating on the bike path. Weddings on wheels. The ultimate worldwide center for roller skating is in Venice, along the oceanfront walk; and for a skater a trip to Venice is a visit to the Holy Land. See the movies *Roller Boogie* and *Skatetown USA* first.

HOW TO SURF IN NEW YORK CITY

Get on board a Broadway express subway train when it isn't too crowded. Stand in the middle of the car, away from the walls. Don't hold on to anything. When the train starts moving, crouch slightly, and try to maintain your balance. Meanwhile, listen to a Beach Boys tape on your Walkman.

SANDBOARDING

An offshoot of snowboarding, which took the principle of surfing away from the beach into the mountains. This returns the idea to the beach. It's easy to do, really—like slalom waterskiing on sand dunes. Got it?

BOOGIE BOARDING

Bodysurfing on a soft foam board. As good an introduction as any to surfing. The boogie board is small and easy to carry. Get used to taking it with you everywhere—to school, work, dinner, the movies.

SKIMBOARDING

As easy as skipping rocks on the water's edge, except that you will be hopping on board for the ride. Be prepared to become very familiar with the surface of the sand.

WINDSURFING

A cross between sailing, surfing, and cult religion. Probably the hardest thing about windsurfing is listening to its promoters and enthusiasts, who attach great zeal to their mission. They can usually be stopped in their tracks with the question "Wait a minute—do I have to get *wet* to do this?"

WARREN MILLER'S SKI FILMS

The major sporting event of the fall season is the local showing of Warren Miller's ski films. Usually shown for one night only, with Warren himself narrating, this is the night on which surfers and other ocean-sports enthusiasts suddenly shift gears and begin thinking winter. This is an important sign, since the usual warnings of winter—leaves turning colors and dropping off trees, for instance—are absent in Southern California. A very traditional event, with much oohing, ahhing, and general hooting going on in the audience. The first down garments of the season are usually spotted at these screenings.

High End Sports

Expensive sports are the best sports because they're the most expensive. Sailing and tennis, for instance, are especially desirable if they involve privately owned boats and tennis courts. And the fact that the skiing in Southern California happens to be very good is beside the point. Skiing is terrific because it is very, very expensive.

In this tradition there are always new twists (novelty combined with expense being the ultimate source of status). The three that you should concentrate on are:

THE PRIVATE TRAINER: He or she comes to your house for individual, daily workout sessions. You should choose your trainer not on the basis of how fit his or her clients are, but rather on the basis of how famous they are.

THE PRIVATE GYM: A room in your house devoted to complex exercise equipment— Universal, for instance, or better still, Nautilus—helps tremendously. Give special consideration to any equipment that is heavily chromed. Extra points for a one-lane lap pool.

THE TRUCK: It looks like a diaper service truck, except that it combines the private gym and private trainer in one. The trainer drives to your house and you work out in a gym inside the truck. The idea is to provide complete privacy. The idea is also to have the truck park right in *front* of your house and to keep the doors *open*, so people can understand how much you want that privacy.

Week 4
SURF 'N' TURF

As a Southern Californian, you have an inalienable right to sun. And you should feel righteously outraged if anyone or anything conspires to deny you your sun.

Hence the annual Festival of Cloud Denial, which usually runs through May and June. As any meteorologist will tell you, these two months happen to be cloudy in Southern California. In fact it can remain consistently overcast for all of this period. Yet every year you will express consternation and hurt disappointment throughout the spring: how dare it not be sunny?

And every spring the newspapers and TV news shows will run pieces on how it's always like that at this time of year, and on how every year Southern Californians act surprised even though they really shouldn't.

But don't let the journalists dissuade you. When a cloudy spring rolls around, show who you really are. Repeat the mystical Cloud Denial Incantation, "Can you believe this weather? I thought it was supposed to be sunny in California."

THE SUN

The sun is a large, hot, yellow, gaseous sphere that, just like the Goodyear blimp, has its home base and is serviced in Southern California (near the 405 freeway) and generally works a route that roughly follows the coastline from

Time in California

Time in Southern California is different from time anywhere else.

In California you will rise early and, usually, go to bed early. Thus, eleven A.M. may be lunchtime, noon may be called midafternoon, and at four thirty P.M. people in your office will ask you, "Why are you still here?"

Also, it is not possible to call, say, New York on business from your office in Southern California. By the time you arrive at work at nine A.M. it is twelve noon in New

Tijuana to Santa Barbara. It is taken into the shop for inspection and refurbishing in May and June most years.

As with the blimp, it is felt to be a stupid idea for anyone to stare at it too long.

York, and everyone has gone to lunch. By the time they return from lunch, it is eleven thirty or twelve o'clock in California, and you have gone to lunch. By the time *you* return from lunch, they've gone home in New York. As a result, communication between New York and Los Angeles is most efficiently conducted by rumor and innuendo.

Time in California is used primarily as a measure of distance, according to the formula $D = T$: distance equals time. Thus a Southern Californian asked how far away he lives will answer "Forty-five minutes." This is, of course, a measure of driving time, and may be affected by the formula $V \propto \frac{1}{CHP}$: velocity is inversely proportional to the number of encounters with the California Highway Patrol.

And there are special kinds of time in California. Tennis time is one form of which there is never a shortage. Special time is usually related to the sun. Peak Tanning Hours, for instance (PTH), or beach parking time, measured not in hours of the day but regulated by signs reading NO PARKING SUNSET TO SUNRISE. Car waxing time is always whenever the sun is past the house, affording the necessary shade, and is always on Sunday.

Becoming Blond

Regardless of your natural coloring, it is your privilege as a new or old Southern Californian to become blond.

You should remember, however, that unless it comes completely naturally to you— without even the help of the sun—*being blond is a responsibility.*

If you turn blond in the sun, you have to remember to maintain the necessary exposure all year round.

If you require certain, shall we say, assistance, you must regulate it carefully, and maintain the proper discretion in denying that you use it. The rumors of certain surfers' using Comet cleanser now appear to have emanated from Australia. (Okay. Okay. We're talking about Sun In here.)

If you require heroic measures to become blond, you must be prepared to deal with sudden baldness.

In any case, you will always insist that it's simply the sun that did it.

Always.

Sunglasses

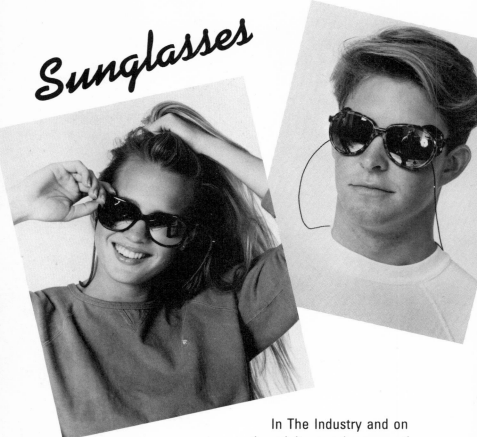

In your zeal to get the California spirit, you may already have bought sunglasses. The instinct is right, but sunglasses alone are not enough. You need to have the correct sunglasses. Let's start with the most basic selection. As you gain confidence, and get used to perpetual twilight, you may experiment further.

In The Industry and on the adult upscale scene, the right sunglasses would be the glamor brands—Porsche, especially, or Polo (with the logo visible, of course).

Outside of The Industry, among the beach crowd and the younger upscale set (the children of Beverly Hills, for example), the choices are different. Following the fashion lead of surfers, the correct glasses to pick would be

Vuarnets (pronounced var-NAYs) or Ray-Ban Wayfarers. By Vuarnets we mean primarily the "cat-eye" style, which may be personalized by a wide range of accessories. The Ray-Ban Wayfarers are an old fifties design recently resurrected, available in black or tortoiseshell. The black is marginally hipper, though both are sufficiently hip. The only accessory appropriate to Wayfarers would be a neck cord.

SUNGLASSES ACCESSORIES

It is always cool to accessorize your sunglasses, so long as the accessories are high-tech, or at least arguably functional. This means no diamond monograms. But starting with the neck cord (de rigueur), there is a spectacular range of options, which may be combined in many exotic arrangements.

Windscreens which slip over the temples of the glasses, clip-on visors, cinch straps for sports—they're all useful, especially in combination. The ultimate high-tech sunglasses are mountaineering glasses, which have leather side blinders, a thin neck cord, and are dark enough to leave you arguably blind.

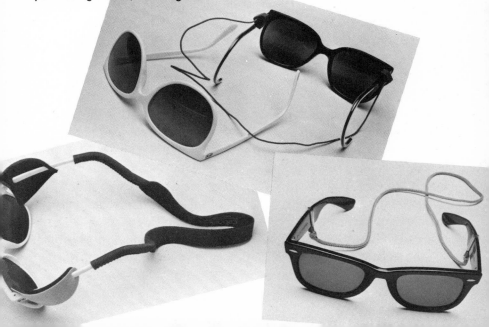

Lotions and Potions

Ultimately the idea is to have such a good, permanent tan that you never need any suntan preparations at all.

But there are a couple of ways to get there in the first place. If you're rich, live in Malibu, and work in The Industry (or all three, which is a pretty likely combination), it's Bain de Soleil.

If you're just your basic cool California kind of person, buy your choice of the Hawaiian Tropic products.

And, for the average, all-American beachgoer, there's always plain old Coppertone, which deserves your support for providing those distinctive yellow oil-drum trash cans which are classic landmarks— "Meet me at the third trash can after the second life-guard stand."

The finishing touch— probably a bit too high-tech for most of you—is a generous coating of pure white zinc oxide on the nose. It's a look that says, "I'm so serious about being out in the sun that I can't afford to mess around, okay?"

Carmex, if you can find it, is what to use on your lips for windburn and chapping, because it comes in a great little white glass jar that, unlike the Chap Stick container, won't allow the contents to run all over everything when the sun hits it.

Swimwear

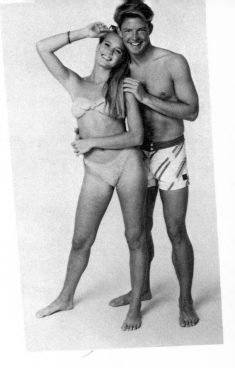

WOMEN

The string bikini is the ideal uniform because it is the easiest to wear. All you need is a perfect body. Now, we have to face facts here—some of you aren't ready for string. In that case you may wear a one-piece, maillot-type suit. But it must be cut exaggeratedly high in the hips, and more so down the front. If you absolutely can't look the way you want in either of these, you may, as a last resort, wear Dolfin shorts and a T-shirt or jersey; just pretend that you are always just about to take them off to reveal a string bikini and a perfect bod. Under no circumstances should you wear any suit that incorporates a little skirt.

MEN

One of California's great sartorial contributions to the world is surf trunks. They are unlined, made of heavyweight fabric to resist abrasion from rocks and sand, and come in millions of patterns formed by assembling different-shaped, different-colored panels. They may be worn quite long on the leg. If you are a surfer, this is your only choice. Surf trunks have gone fully new wave lately, and color combinations like black and pink have gained favor. If you are not a surfer, you can wear running shorts; racing suits are favored by the hard-core swingles scene, Venice Beach bodybuilders, and Hollywood.

And over any of these—including the Dolfin shorts—

you should wear OPs or Bermudas on your way to the beach even if what you have on underneath is perfectly adequate as shorts. The beach is the one place where Southern Californians observe the layered look.

THE BEACH AS ZOO

The beach is exceptionally crowded on summer weekends. Do not show yourself to be an outsider by complaining (except about parking). Those crowds are the *reason* you go to the beach.

THE BEACH POLICE

Those guys in the navy-blue OP shorts, the light-blue jerseys, and running shoes, going around on cruiser bicycles, carrying walkie-talkies and nightsticks, are the real thing, so pay attention to them. *Do not say, "You're a policeman??!!"* as they attempt to escort you to that big Ford Bronco with the official seal on the door.

BEACH BUSINESSES

People sell all manner of things on the beach. It is acceptable to buy novelty ices, or sunglasses, or T-shirts, or beach towels at the beach, but please do not let the sun daze you into bringing home sequined head antennas, any electronic equipment made by Somy, Tanasonic, or Sinyo, invisible-dog novelties, or kites that require more than two hundred hours training to fly.

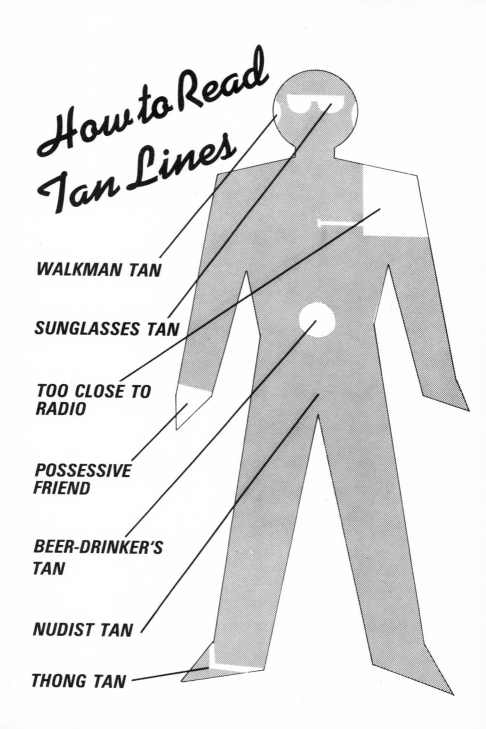

ATTITUDE

If you can surf at all, surfing must be the most important thing in your life. A good surf report on the radio or TV can instantly preempt any planned daily activity. Whole high school French classes have been known to empty out halfway through the period because the classroom happened to have a good view of the beach. There are construction companies that only do work on bad surf days.

Those surfers sitting in the beach parking lot on the hoods of their cars, gazing out to sea, are as unbudgeable as the Mount Rushmore monument; they are waiting for the right set. Please don't ask them to vacate their parking spots.

Aggression is the new keynote for surfers. The advent of shorter, more maneuverable boards (with as many as five fins) permits aggressive ("aggro") style surfing, and the increasing crowding of limited space for surfing has turned peaceful surfers into territorial monsters, fighting to keep intruders out of locals-only areas. If you are a surfer from the Valley, in particular, you had better be damn good if you don't want to risk attack. "Vals go home" is the "Remember the Alamo" of surfing. And the key words used to describe *good* surfing are straight from guerrilla warfare: *shred, slash and burn, thrash.* The image of the mellow, laid-back surfer is a thing of the past.

PERSONAL STYLE

The idea of the surfer as a kind of a low-key hippie is about dead, too. The correct look is extremely well groomed. Sun-bleached hair should be well trimmed and may range from a Kennedy-era style through rockabilly to crew cut or punk, but in any case must be freshly cut at all times.

The old cutoff jeans and *huaraches* are gone, too, replaced by modified prep clothes in bold pastels. Bermuda shorts, sleeveless T-shirts, and hepster sunglasses have taken their places alongside the still-popular OP shorts and long-sleeved T-shirts. The ultimate compliment to a surfer about his appearance is "Very *G.Q.*"

When you ask a surfer if he ever considers doing anything else, he says, "Sure—I'd like to model."

Surfboards, wet suits, and other paraphernalia are now produced or decorated in high-tech and new-wave designs and colors; the peacock has landed at the beach. Surfers can be seen arguing fiercely about the relative merits of the airbrushed paint jobs on their boards.

WHERE TO SURF

Sorry—the best spots will not be revealed here. Your own ideal spot should be almost totally inaccessible. Preferably somewhere far down Mexico's Baja Peninsula, requiring four-wheel drive and two complete changes of tires to reach. You should talk about it endlessly, but not reveal its whereabouts.

SURF MUSIC

There are two categories. The more recent is surf punk—raw, slam-dancing stuff. The more obscure and short-lived (and violent) the band, the better. Then there is the grand tradition, which includes the Beach Boys and Jan and Dean for vocal music but is made up primarily of the best sixties instrumental sounds. The tapes in your car should include the Ventures, Dick Dale's guitar sounds, the Chantays (they did "Pipeline"), and the Surfaris ("Wipeout") for starters.

WHY JANIE CAN'T SURF

Girls can't surf. Okay, *some* of them can, and have earned respect for it, but most just don't. In particular, a surfer's girlfriend must not even try. She should instead devote herself to waiting on the beach or in the parking lot for her surfer to come in, so they can have the standard argument:

"You weren't watching. I was shredding on that last wave and you weren't looking!"
"I was too."

HOW TO RUN LIKE A SURFER

Just run as though you're paddling a surfboard. Never let your arms swing farther forward than your hips. Snap your wrists back in little flipper motions.

WHAT IS SEX WAX?

Mr. Zogs (*sic*) Original Sex Wax ("Never Spoils; the Best for Your Stick") is the classic surfboard wax (used, that is, to provide traction for the feet). Sex Wax T-shirts (especially the long-sleeved ones) are crucial to your collection.

DISASTER

The mark of the newcomer to Southern California is anxiety over natural disaster, especially earthquake.

Recent arrivals have plenty of questions: Where is the fault line? What do I do if an

earthquake hits? What's it like? Can I get where I'm going without passing under or over any highway overpasses?

But these worries fade with time. Instead of thinking, "Gee, there still hasn't been an earthquake—doesn't that mean that the pressure's *really* building up for a big one?" the acclimated Southern Californian thinks, "See? I've lived here X years without ever feeling one, so I guess they don't really matter."

So—to be truly Californian—*do not* follow any of the safety precautions printed clearly in the front of your phone book. *Don't* store water. *Don't* stockpile canned food. *Don't* have battery-operated radios and lights on hand. *Don't* learn how to turn off your gas supply. *Don't* have an emergency plan.

Do make occasional jokes about "the big one," but not too often. *Do* hang heavy pictures or objects above your bed where they could fall and hurt you. (Mirrored ceilings are especially appropriate in this context.)

THE FIRST COMPLETELY ACCURATE EARTHQUAKE TIMETABLE EVER

First month in California: Great fear, constant concern. Panic when driving under bridges and overpasses. Attempts made to stockpile emergency supplies.

Sixth month in California: Fear abates. Stockpiles gradually used up for other emergencies, like running short of something at a party.

Twelfth month in California: Able to joke about earthquakes. Occasional references to something not really mattering, since someday we'll all fall into the Pacific. Ha ha ha.

Twenty-fourth month in California: Should have felt a little tremor or two by now, leaving one convinced that earthquakes aren't any big deal after all.

Thirty-sixth month in California: Plans under way to build vacation house on San Andreas Fault.

Sliding into Home

Of course when it finally does rain in Southern California, it rains like crazy, frequently resulting in disastrous flooding and mud slides in the hills. How should you, as a Californian, respond to this?

If your concern is safety, stay away from easily eroded hillsides and flood basins when finding a place to live. But if your concern is simply to behave in the most Southern Californian way possible (and it should be), respond the same way you would to fire. *Continue to build in the same place.* Or build on an even steeper hillside. Cantilever your house farther out; shore it up with longer stilts. Prove that you're not ashamed to be a Southern Californian.

A SIMPLE TEST OF SOUTHERN CALIFORNIANISM

You are visiting friends who live in a stilt-house high up on the side of a very steep canyon. You go out on the terrace, which shakes and wobbles beneath you. Beneath the terrace there is nothing except a rocky hillside a few hundred feet down. You wouldn't put your stereo on a shelf this flimsy. You:

A. Find an excuse to leave quickly.
B. Stay in the part of the house closest to the ground.
C. Ask if they could use a roommate.

If you answered A, you still need a lot of work. If you answered B, you're getting there. If you answered C, congratulations. You're a Southern Californian already and don't have to read any further.

DROUGHT

Southern Californians have in the past successfully demonstrated their ability to conserve water most efficiently in times of drought (which can occur with regularity).

Here, for your information, is a list of water conservation measures that you will adopt when necessary, starting with sacrifices made in times of mild shortages and working up to heroic measures.

The first thing you will give up is water for drinking. At least tap water. After all, as a Southern Californian you should be drinking bottled water by now, anyhow.

Next you can give up bathing water. Rely on dips in the Jacuzzi or pool for hygiene.

As things get tougher you may have to cut back on watering your grounds. Better yet, simply replant with cactus and succulents, which are what should be there anyway.

Finally, as the drought reaches its more dire proportions, come the Last Three Things to Go.

1. Water for car washing.

(Keep the car covered. Don't go anywhere. Lick it clean, if necessary.)

2. Pool and Jacuzzi water. Keep the pool covered to prevent evaporation. Move it out of the sun.

3. Water for hosing down your driveway. Always the last to go. Californians believe they have a very special dispensation never to have to use a broom or rake or (worst of all) to bend over to clear dust and leaves out of their driveways. This can only be accomplished by hosing down, or by the application of a leaf blower, which requires a professional gardener or handyman to operate, unless you want to be strapped to a very disreputable-looking internal combustion engine.

FIRE

Where else but in Southern California could a fire raging out of control for the third day and consuming thirty thousand acres including residential land be covered by the TV news *after* a story about the nice weather at the beach? Where else would the magnitude of such a fire really be brought home to the public not by reporting the number of families left homeless but by the value of the real estate (thus reports of "sixteen houses lost in Anaheim including portions of an exclusive enclave of homes worth $650,000 to $1,000,000")?

This doesn't mean that the major brush fires that occur almost every fall when the hot Santa Ana winds blow off the desert across bone-dry brush are taken lightly. It's just that they occur so regularly that there isn't much new to say about them. As a nearly native Californian you must shoulder your burden and be prepared to rebuild in exactly the same danger zones. You may arm yourself with a few offhand phrases: "We just couldn't give up the view!" "We had been meaning to clear out that brush, anyway." "What am I supposed to do—move to *Ohio*?"

Week 5

ROOM AND BOARD

S *ince you are well on your way to adapting your life-style, it is time to adapt that place where you do most of your living—your home. If you spend more time away from home than at home, that must be changed now, too. From now on you will entertain at home, take meetings at home, and exercise at home.*

You say you're living in a pre-Revolutionary Connecticut farmhouse? A high-rise in Chicago? A plantation in Mississippi? Don't worry. Your house can be adapted to the California mode.

If you already live in California but fear that your house is somehow not sufficiently Californian, that can be corrected.

Here's how.

How to Make Your Home More Californian, Wherever It Is

TEXTURED WALLS AND COTTAGE-CHEESE CEILINGS

The interior materials of choice. No smooth surfaces, please. These materials cover up all manner of imperfections in construction, of course, but they have become so popular that you will want them even in your well-constructed house. The cottage-cheese ceiling has a tendency to shed whenever a truck goes past the house.

CERAMIC TILE COUNTERS IN KITCHEN AND BATHROOM

Did you think Formica was the material of the future? Forget it. The California passion for anything arts-and-crafts has deemed ceramic tiles your choice for kitchen counters. Sure, they crack, and dirt gets in between them and they don't provide a usable flat surface, but tilework is a *craft*!

STUCCO

The outside material of choice. Sprayed on in a day. It's light, it's cheap, and it looks like stucco. Hide that embarrassing brickwork, those old-looking clapboards.

DIAGONAL WOOD PANELING

Start by installing this in your sauna. Then maybe accent the front of your house with diagonal redwood. Then perhaps the living room and the kitchen. The nice thing about diagonal paneling is that when your house is tilted by an earthquake, it will end up looking *better than before.*

CONCRETE BLOCK WALL AROUND HOUSE

Southern California houses are usually built on small lots, and to maximize land usage and provide privacy, a concrete block wall may be constructed around it. This is not considered ugly, as it would be elsewhere. After all, concrete blocks are almost like adobe, right? And they can always be covered with stucco.

STAINED GLASS

Crafts strike again. It is crucial to have some piece of stained glass in at least one window of your house. It doesn't have to be good stained glass at all, by the way. Favorite subjects include rainbows, bunches of grapes, sunrises, sunsets, and rainbows again. Tell everyone that you found the piece of glass at the artist's own studio just off Highway One in Big Sur. This is very impressive.

NEUTRALS AND NATURALS

The idea is to make your house look *restful*, so your color scheme should be in shades of white, tan, beige, café au lait, cream, linen, and, for a little accent, off-white. Some bamboo poles in a giant terra-cotta vase, some cocoa matting on the floor. Coffee tables made of bleached tree-trunk sections.

THE CAR DISPLAY

You will want to construct a semicircular driveway cutting across your front lawn for the purpose of displaying your fine collection of cars. A couple of low spotlights for drama, and one or two high floodlights to fill in the shadows should complete the image.

SPRINKLERS

It doesn't matter what you have for a lawn or garden; install a built-in sprinkler system. Even in a window box.

FIVE-DIGIT HOUSE NUMBERS

A Californian tradition. Just add on to your own.

OAK FURNITURE

Ball-and-claw tables, pressed-back chairs, rolltop desks—if it's oak it *must* be beautiful. Southern California is peppered with stores which sell nothing but oak furniture. "Dear, I'm going down to Oak World for another ice-chest/TV swivel stand. Need anything?"

THE NEW PASTELS

A new twist on the neutral California color scheme. The new pastels are coral and turquoise. Sort of faded HoJo, very new-wave. Paint the outside of your house these colors and proclaim to the world your new, post-modernist sensibilities.

BRIAN DAVIS FLOWER POSTERS

A sort of post-deco effect; paintings of brilliantly colored tropical flowers against black backgrounds, with the artist's name, Brian Davis, printed across the bottom. A Southern California certificate of occupancy.

A ROCKET MAN

This man walks around and around your house with a gas-powered, Buck Rogers rocket pack (actually a leaf blower), blowing loose leaves and clippings all the way out to the street. Hang up your rakes—they scratch the ground, anyway.

SHAG CARPETING

Everywhere. Landlords will actually apologize for the bare hardwood parquet, and promise to install shag immediately. The major colors are electric blue, avocado, harvest gold, and orange.

Signs of Home

Your house is supposed to advertise your wealth, good taste, or bad taste (of equal merit) all by itself, but it is considered wise in Southern California to help it along with subtle, semiotic reminders. Here are the most popular.

FOR SALE SIGN

Every house in Southern California is for sale. You will want a big sign with the logo of the real estate agent hanging from a post on your front lawn. Even if you don't plan to move, you should set an unreasonably high price and register with the broker, because the *right* real estate agency in your neighborhood conveys status. Many brokers "won't touch" anything under, say, a million dollars, so you can see the benefits of such an association.

SIGN CALLING ATTENTION TO AMENITIES

Under the guise of providing warning, you can advertise your home's luxuries. CAUTION: ELECTRICALLY OPERATED GATES SWING OUT, for instance. Or PLEASE LOOK AT TV CAMERA

WHEN ANNOUNCING YOURSELF. Or PLEASE DO NOT WALK ON PUTTING GREEN. And inside, CAUTION: WET BAR.

SECURITY SIGNS

These are small enameled-metal plaques that stud the perimeter of the lawn, and appear again next to doors and windows. They bear the name of the alarm system manufacturer, which should give the thoughtful burglar some idea of which type of system he will have to disconnect, and should also alert him that there is something on the premises worth protecting.

The ultimate in these signs, especially popular in areas like Trousdale Estates,

is the additional sign attached just below the alarm sign, which reads ARMED RESPONSE. This of course warns the burglar that he had better arrive armed, too.

POISON WARNINGS

People who don't want domestic animals messing with their landscaping have hit upon a terrific scheme: signs are available (and are widely used) which read WARNING! THESE PREMISES HAVE BEEN TREATED WITH CHEMICALS WHICH MAY BE POISONOUS TO PETS. Usually there are children laughing and rolling about on these lawns, which should answer the charge that Southern Californians treat their children like pets.

Real Estate/ Unreal Estate

More than anywhere else, the real estate agent is an esteemed member of society in Southern California. Sporting a gold Rolex, or a Cartier

Santos, and driving a Rolls or Mercedes, he or she makes periodic visits to almost everyone, because in Southern California, *almost everyone's house is for sale.* Just in case. Just in case that rich Arab with the car trunk full of cash (sort of the tooth fairy of the adult world) decides that *your* house would be the ideal gift for his twelve-year-old daughter.

Thus, everyone should (and does) know the lingo of real estate. In particular there are certain amenities peculiar to Southern California that you should know, and should look for in choosing, building, describing in print, or improving your own house.

PREVIOUS TENANTS

Who lived in your house before you? It could add value to your house. Find an old Map of the Stars' Homes and check for yours. If necessary, fake it. But never claim that yours was a star's sole residence, because there are always counterclaims for other home-owners. Tell people that, say, Clark Gable used this house during the filming of *Gone With the Wind*; or if it is a house too small to be a plausible star home, say that it was "the love nest of Mary Pickford and Douglas Fairbanks in the twenties."

GATED SECURITY SYSTEM

It doesn't matter whether or not you have anything worth protecting. You really ought to have an electrically operated gate at the end of your driveway, augmented by an intercom at driver's window-level and a closed circuit TV camera.

N/S TENNIS COURT

Don't be puzzled by this cryptic description in the real estate ads. The north-slash-south tennis court is one situated to give both sides the same advantage or disadvantage from the sun. If you don't have room for an n/s tennis court, why bother to build one at all?

BLACK-BOTTOM POOL

Not a place where a 1920s dance craze is performed underwater, but a pool painted black inside, instead of light blue-green. Very chic—it looks like a pond, or reflecting pool. Also, it is very hard to see how far away the bottom is when diving in, adding an element of excitement.

340° VIEW

What are they gonna do, bring a protractor? Claim a view whenever possible. If buyers complain that they can't see it, tell them that it gets much better after the canyon fires in the fall.

RANCHES

Any second home in the country that is not distinctly a beach house or a ski lodge may be called a ranch. Do not be fooled by the Ponderosa. What is called a ranch in Southern California may well be called a shack in the rest of the country.

LANAI

A fancy Hawaiian word for porch.

MAIDS' ROOMS

It is best to have more maids' rooms than family bedrooms; you may therefore want to consider renaming some rooms.

BHPO

This means Beverly Hills Post Office. Not quite in Beverly Hills, that is, but you get to use a Beverly Hills mailing address. Value by association is important in real estate here, thus also Bev. Hls. Adj. (Beverly Hills Adjacent), and apartments and developments with names like Bel-Air-View, Laguna-by-the-Freeway, and so on.

THE MALIBU BEACH HOUSE

Also, do not be fooled by the term "Malibu Beach House." This, too, can be a little shack. While parts of Malibu are quite grand, the average Malibu Beach house—and these are the million-dollar houses we're talking about here—looks like something you pull out to the middle of a lake in winter for ice fishing. It is six feet from the highway on one side, meaning it can take fifteen minutes just to exit from your own garage when the traffic is really moving, and not much farther from the water's edge on the other side, meaning it can collapse in heavy surf. This is all very, very desirable.

ODD HOUSING

California may well be the last stronghold of the sort of eccentric housing that mushroomed in the 1960s. Homemade geodesic domes, yurts, orange-crate shacks, odd solar arrangements, tepees—they all have a cherished place in Southern California real estate. Especially when it was discovered that the land upon which many were built became exceptionally valuable in the recent real estate booms, making millionaires of hermits and resorts of communes. So to own such a home is a sign of great wisdom. It says that you knew about the big boom all along.

FANTASY HOUSING

Southern California is the residential Disneyland, where everyone gets to live his or her own fantasy through the home. Thus, neighborhoods where a Norman keep stands next to a lunar module, next to a Venetian palazzo, next to Hansel and Gretel's house, next to the Petit Trianon.

Jacuzzis and Hot Tubs

Basically, you have two choices. The kind that's blue inside—in concrete, molded Fiberglas or plastic—and the redwood tub.

The redwood tub looks like part of a big wine barrel. It should be installed in a redwood deck behind the house, with a little redwood trellis over it hung with ferns in baskets. It's a bit sixties, somehow, or perhaps a bit Marin County.

The other kind—more often called a Jacuzzi even though Jacuzzi is just one brand name, is more sleek and modern, and definitely more upscale. Frequently it is installed as an adjunct to the swimming pool. It may have a light in it, underwater, which it is in poor taste to turn on suddenly when the Jacuzzi is being used at night.

JACUZZI ETIQUETTE

DO NOT take off all your clothes if no one else in the tub is doing so.

DO offer your guests wine or pot in the tub, but only after warning them that they take effect much more quickly in the hot, swirling water.

DON'T pee—it doesn't dissipate the way it does in a big pool. They'll see it.

DON'T dive. There is no deep end. It is NOT CUTE to put the cat into the whirlpool.

DON'T eat in the Jacuzzi. The action of the water will turn anything you drop into a blender drink instantly.

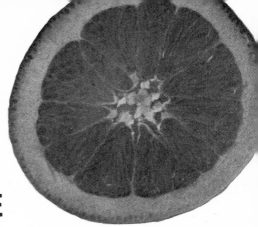

Food

THE UBIQUITOUS ORANGE SLICE

The parsley of the coast, orange slices are easily the favorite garnish in all California restaurants. Everything from sushi to guacamole may be deftly punctuated with a quarter-inch slice of orange, which, miraculously, *always appears to come from the center of the orange*. This leads to the widespread speculation that special food-service-only oranges are grown, in the shape of salamis.

GRAVEL-GRAINED BREAD

The more grains in the bread, the better in Southern California. The most popular, ten-grain bread, is just the tip of the loaf. Words like *whole, cracked, un*anything *(unbleached, unground, unshelled)* are always believed to signal better nutrition in grain products. That sandwiches tend to crumble into a pile of organic gravel before they are half eaten is irrelevant. And even those all-American spun-sugar classics, hot-dog and hamburger buns, are preferred here in what is called with some condescension to the white variety, "wheat" bread.

WHAT, ME DRINK?

From left: Tequila Sunrise, club soda with lime, Margarita, white wine spritzer, Old Faithful.

NOUVELLE CALIFORNIA CUISINE

In California's nouvelle cuisine, the idea is to take the smallest possible food and to worry it to death. The piece of kiwi fruit is shown here for nostalgic reasons: not only is the kiwi a cliché of nouvelle cuisine, it is also a cliché to point out that the kiwi is a cliché.

HEALTH

The word "health" is a magic buzzword that probably has no meaning but makes you feel better anyway when associated with something you are ordering; thus "health bread," "health salad," "health steak."

CHILIBURGERS

From now on, when you order hamburgers from a hamburger stand, you will have to specify if you *don't* want chili on them. Actually, the chili is a sort of bland mush, but hell—it's traditional. The all-time original (and best) chiliburger stand is called Tommy's, and it's at 2575 West Beverly in Los Angeles. Its popularity has given rise to an immense industry—the pseudo-Tommy's stands. Every variation of the name is used: Tom's, Tomy's, Timmy's, Tammy's, Tommie's; usually with a number following the name (Tom's #5). Many of these places are pretty good, too. The best item is usually the double chili cheeseburger.

SPROUTS

China has rice. Ireland has potatoes. And Southern California, sprouts. They appear everywhere. In salads, of course, but also in sandwiches, casseroles, even desserts. The classic California sprout is alfalfa, with mung and soy running close behind. Natural foods stores stock even more

varieties, giving rise to the five-sprout salad, which means five varieties, not five sprouts.

HERB TEA

Teas made with products other than tea are very much part of the mainstream in the California beverage world, and it is entirely reasonable to be surprised and annoyed when a classic French restaurant fails to have your favorite, Red Zinger. Teas made with hibiscus, rose thorns, whatever, are presumed to be far more healthful than old-fashioned tea, because the latter contains caffeine, which, as we all know, makes you *hyper* and *unmellow*.

SUSHI

You must develop an extensive knowledge of the varieties of Japanese raw fish dishes that are readily available throughout the Southland. You should have chosen your favorite sushi bar, and should talk about it at great length. Your own favorite sushi chef is a confidant and friend on a par with your barber or hairdresser or psychiatrist, and you should tip him accordingly.

Southern California sushi chefs are traditionally outrageously cheerful, and a trip to the sushi bar can be a valuable restorative. California sushi bars are much louder than those elsewhere, with much shouting back and forth across the room. They are also the home of the California roll, so named because it contains avocado. Try not to be someone else's guest at a sushi bar, because your host will bore you to death explaining sushi, even if you know all about it. It's traditional.

CERTIFIED MILK

It's raw, it's unpasturized, it's Californian.

THE ULTIMATE CALIFORNIA SANDWICH

Tomato, sprouts, avocado, cheddar and Monterey Jack cheeses, lettuce or spinach on whole-grain bread with mayonnaise (natural only, please). Garnished with an orange slice on the plate.

CHIPS AND SALSA

Peanuts or popcorn or pretzels in a bar? Unthinkable. The classic Southern California munchy food is freshly made tortilla chips and a big bowl of fresh salsa (tomatoes and hot chilies, basically, with *cilantro,* lime, and/or onions added according to the private recipe of each establishment). Proper salsa makes your eyes water and your mouth burn like crazy. The only cure is to take another big scoop of salsa (it's cooling, too) immediately. Always ask for a second dish soon, or you may be suspected of being an outsider.

AVOCADOS

Not a luxury but a necessity here. You should always have several at home, because it takes a few days of sitting on the counter for them to ripen. "But there's no *avocado* in this chicken salad sandwich!" is a reasonable complaint. Guacamole is the onion soup dip of the southwest. During a recent bumper crop the avocado industry promoted their product as an excellent dog food.

Drive-In Culture

Since your car is becoming the single greatest source of pleasure in your life, why get out of it at all? To this end Southern California is without doubt the world leader in drive-in services. Apart from the more familiar drive-in services, like movies, bank tellers, and gas stations, California offers some novelties.

The traditional drive-in restaurant—waitresses on roller skates, and so forth—has been replaced by the "drive-thru" (the preferred spelling), at most fast-food outlets. The trick is to *memorize the menu in advance,* in order to avoid one of the great Southern California embarrassments—hemming and hawing while cars are lined up behind you waiting for you to place your order with the disembodied, amplified voice coming out of the illuminated color picture of the cheeseburger.

Southern California also provides drive-in church services, drive-thru dry cleaners, drive-thru video rentals, drive-thru supermarkets (order by phone, pick up by car), and drive-thru zoos. But the spot closest to your heart must be reserved for the Alta-Dena dairy/gas drive-ins (that's right—just what it sounds like—a fill-up, a quart of skimmed, and some cottage cheese). And, for true believers, Sunset Boulevard's combination car wash/wine store.

Week 6

MIND TRIPS

"But how can I California?" you ask. "There's so much to do, so much to think about, so much to remember! How will I ever get it right?"

Mellow out, *man. Don't get so* hyper. Go with the flow.

See? You're beginning to catch on already. But don't go too far; don't be fooled by the stereotype of the relaxed Californian. In actuality, mellow is more an ideal than a practice. Californians are just about as excitable as anyone else; it's just that they think about relaxation more, and talk about it more. It's important that you understand the terms.

Mellow *is a state you will achieve on certain occasions, usually aided by good wine, good music, a good sunset, good friends, good lovemaking, good vibes, or of course hard drugs. Eventually you snap out of it.*

Laid back *is a more permanent personality trait, and it means blessed with natural serenity, when used in its most positive* sense. Otherwise, it is a euphemism for "chronically lazy" or "permanently enfeebled by drugs or by surfboard contact to the head, or both."

Vacant *is what easterners tend to call either of these conditions, and* hyper *is what* mellow, laid back Californians *call those easterners, usually with heartfelt pity.*

A Southern Californian encountering for the first time the rapid speech characteristic of, for instance, New York City, may ask, "What are you on?" If this happens to you, please try not to respond impulsively. It is not an insult. The Californian just thinks it may be interesting to try some of whatever it is. You should answer, "Ginseng."

SOME THINGS SOUTHERN CALIFORNIANS DO GET EXCITED ABOUT:

Tranquilizers
Isolation Tanks
Hot Tubs
Massage
Good Surf
Sushi

SOME THINGS SOUTHERN CALIFORNIANS DON'T GET EXCITED ABOUT:

Earthquakes
Where You Went to Prep School
Staying Up Late and Going to Studio 54

Go est, Young Man

You have, no doubt, already heard about est, the two-weekend "seminars training" designed by Werner Erhard to "transform your ability to experience living." Perhaps you have come to the conclusion that it is a big joke, or a dangerous cult, or just some weird fringe activity that involves people you don't know and never will know.

Well, be prepared to be surprised, because in Southern California plenty of people you know have been through est and they take it very, very seriously. Without changing your convictions about est, you should understand that there is a code among non-est Californians about how to treat people who have taken, as they call it, "the training."

1. You are not supposed to crack jokes about est; only est graduates can do that, and then the jokes are supposed to be enlightening. The correct response isn't just to laugh, but also to say "Isn't that wonderful."

2. When an est trainee tells you, "Thank you for sharing," he means he is glad to have heard your opinion, even if that opinion was expressed like a fist to the face.

3. Werner Erhard may be the only true, living genius. Don't bother trying to argue with this. **3a.** Refer to him as "Werner."

4. You can never tell when someone in a group has been in est; think before you speak.

5. Don't ask why Werner Erhard changed his name from John Paul Rosenberg. It just isn't done.

6. The generous use of the epithet "asshole" is an important part of the est training. When you are called this, please say "Thank you for sharing."

7. If you ask if it's true that there are long stretches during the training when you aren't allowed to go to the bathroom, you will be told that you are "missing the point."

8. If you ask what really goes on in the seminars, and really dig hard enough, you will be told that it would be unfair to describe the experience in words.

9. Nonetheless, you will be encouraged, if you express the slightest interest, to try it for yourself. It can't be described in direct terms, to be sure, but you will be assured that it will change your life. Well, actually, "your ability to experience living." Get it?

10. "Getting it" is the est equivalent of being born again, and should not be confused with "getting some."

11. Est people like to know your first name and then like to use it a whole lot. To help themselves remember, they wear big first-name tags at their gatherings. Sometimes they forget to take these off when they go out to eat.

Behavior Tips

GIVING SPACE

A quick look at real estate values will tell you that space in Southern California is at a premium. Yet you will observe that people here are always either asking for space from others, or offering to give it away. And if you are astute, you may have guessed that there are really two kinds of space.

That's right. There is space, and space. The first kind refers either to geographic space (of which there is plenty in Southern California, but which is also occupied by plenty of Californians) or outer space (which is also occupied by many Californians).

The second kind—the kind you give—is far less tangible, but equally valuable. It has to do with loosening the reins on another person, with giving him some independence; but more important, it is a catchall California euphemism.

Thus, when Southern

Californians say "I need more space," they really mean anything from "I love you but you're cramping my style just the teensiest bit" to "Buzz off," or even "Would you just shut up and wait outside in the car?"

And when they say "I'd like to give you some more space," they really mean anything from "I love you but I'm afraid I may be cramping your style" to "I wish you'd just get the hell out of my life, dirt bag."

Having a Nice Day

Admit it.

Before you came to Southern California you thought, "Everyone's going to tell me to have a nice day and it's going to make me crazy." Then you got here and discovered that you were only partly right. It doesn't make you crazy. In fact, you are starting to like it, and before you know it you'll be returning the sentiment.

The big shock is this: Everyone actually seems to *care* if you have a nice day. They're happy. They want you to be happy, too. What's wrong with that? Being cheerful in public is infectious.

And probably the biggest shock of all will come when you are forced to stifle that smarty-pants answer after the highway patrol officer who has just ticketed you for driving thirty-seven miles over the speed limit wishes, as a parting gift, that you "have a nice day." The ticket was strictly business, after all, and why leave on a sour note?

Have a nice day!

In Southern California, religions, therapies, belief systems, and other karma may be found listed in catalogs, calendars, and magazines with a startling thoroughness and variety. However odd you may find these Sears catalogs of the spirit, it is important to remember one thing.

It is in extremely poor form—very non–Southern Californian—to mock or challenge anyone else's system.

Because nobody should force a belief system on you, we are providing a sample catalog here, allowing you to choose your own. And, of course, you are always free to change. It is perfectly natural, in Southern California, to go through several systems in a very short time.

The Wholistic Hole/ The Holistic Whole

A sourcebook of New Age activities and verbiage related to integrating the whole human person with his/her creative/spiritual development in a nonsexist context of the one-world community of growth/sharing/potential and oneness.

Printed on recyclable paper without any animal fats whatsoever.

LISTINGS
SUNDAY

AUTOMOBILE REPAIR THROUGH ACUPUNCTURE

Beginner, intermediate, and advanced techniques will be discussed for holistic rejuvenation of the automobile—Volkswagen to Mercedes—through ancient Chinese methods. Bring your own needles, please. We will find the cars on the street. 12 noon, Shree Bhagwhag Center and Lube Bay. $3.00 donation requested.

FREE WORKSHOP

For anyone interested in having a good personality, more money, great looks, a strong and disease-free physique, lots of friends, a terrific job, inner peace, strong fingernails, a good apartment at a reasonable rent, the respect of your pets, and a 75-watt Onkyo stereo at a once-in-a-lifetime price. Stereotech Electronics, Century City store only, 9:00 A.M.–5:00 P.M. today only. MC, Visa, Amex accepted.

I HAVE FOUND AN HERB

growing behind my tool shed that takes the place of all food and drink, makes you feel younger and look younger, is NOT sexist or violent, and is nonnarcotic, I think. Send $2.00 for more information. Floyd All-One-God-Persons, General Delivery, Topanga.

WHAT IF THEY GAVE A WAR

and nobody came? Send $5.00 to Floyd All-One-God-Persons, General Delivery, Topanga.

I HAVE YOUR DAUGHTER but

will not harm her if you send $15.95 to me. Floyd All-One-God-Persons, General Delivery, Topanga.

THE WORLD-RENOWNED MYSTIC DEBBI LAUGHING-HYENA SUNFLOWER (formerly Deborah

Kaplan) will be channeling the energies of the animals at the San Diego Zoo into a sculpture for presentation to Messrs. Reagan and Andropov or for the NASA guys to take

on the space shuttle, which-
ever will stop war forever. All
day today, near the ostriches.
Please, no photographs while
Debbi is channeling.

MONDAY

COUPLES AND THREE-SOMES SEXUALITY CLINIC

Learn self-expression through
controlled orgasm, also the
nonorgasm orgasm and a
demonstration of how the
erotic can be integrated with
the body-mind continuum on
an astral plane to produce one
world free of pestilence. Day
care for the children or they
can watch, too. Preregister
now. Box 157, Ojai, CA.

FACELIFTS THROUGH TAROT
are here now. Dr. Ubu Mobubu,
author of "The Cosmic Way
to a Taller Self," will speak, or
gesture. Sheraton Ballroom,
Laguna. 8:00 P.M. sharp.

MARK-MICHAEL-KENNETH is
back! With slides of his trip to
the Godhead. World University,
156792 Hollywood Boulevard,

THIS IS A PICTURE OF A NORMAL APPENDIX.

THIS IS A PICTURE OF *YOUR* APPENDIX WHICH WE GOT FROM YOUR DOCTOR.

Yours is all full of disgusting junk because you don't eat right, breathe right, or think right. **THE KEY TO YOUR WHOLE BEING IS IN YOUR APPENDIX AND YOU'RE LETTING IT GO TO POT.** We can realign your appendix by changing your diet, your exercise, and your personal beliefs to our own. Let us try at no risk to you. **THE ORANGE COUNTY APPENDICENTER®** Harbor Blvd., Anaheim. Across from Disneyland.

3rd floor rear. Knock loud—bell out of order. 6:15 A.M. $1.00 donation requested.

HAVE YOU EVER CONSIDERED HOW YOU LOOK FROM BEHIND?

Many of us are unaware that our whole bodies are not integrated in a harmonious state because we can't see ourselves from behind. I can see you from behind and I want to tell you how you look. Dr. Carla Jung (no relation), Ventura Blvd., Encino. Call for appointment.

TUESDAY

CHANT WITH US!

"Shiva Riva Sargent Shriver. Whee Bang Reno, Reno, Reno. Honda, not-Honda. Honda, not-Honda. Honda, not-Honda. Moo-ooo-oooh." If this experience has changed your life, come to our picnic to learn more. Vegetarian, of course. MacArthur Park, noon. Sponsored by the Church of the Vacuum.

BREATHING WORKSHOP

Many people are not really living because they do not breathe. Together we will learn the in-out technique that has unlocked the secret of life for thousands. Ken and Ken Maxiburger, licensed inhalologist and exhalologist, respectively. Windbag Retreat, Topanga Canyon.

FORGET ABOUT ROLFING, CHIROPRACTIC, YOGA etc. Our vibrators provide deep, penetrating massage and are made exclusively by women. $19.95 each for 7" model; $29.95 each for 12" model. Special orders welcome. Noli Me Tangere, Hollywood and Vine.

The Healing Worm

BOOKSTORE

Specializing in Cosmic and New Age Comic Books and Adult Reading and Viewing Materials, artfully displayed in a nonnegative setting with soft lights, incense, and very soft-spoken employees with bare feet.

Browse all you want, but please buy a 50¢ admission token. Open 24 hours. On the Sunset Strip, Hollywood.

WEDNESDAY

NO WHOLISTIC/ HOLISTIC ACTIVITIES TODAY DUE TO BANK HOLIDAY

THURSDAY

SAND WORSHIP CAN FREE THE LITTLE BIRD IN YOU

A metaphysical approach to a geophysical problem, now taught by masters of the perceived word abiding at the center of the known/unknown universe. Also cheese. The Singing Light Center, Oxnard. 7:30 P.M.

COLONIC IRRIGATION IS THE KEY TO EVERYTHING IN THE WORLD. Please let us help you to flush out the bad and flush in the new. We use Perrier water only, and have a money-back guarantee.

Please—we like doing this, really we do. Please. Rancho Cucamonga Colonic College, Rancho Cucamonga.

CARING, DREAMS, PRIMAL, TOGETHER, POLARITY, non-threatening, creativity, relax, touch, homeopathic, insight, Baba, alignment, vegetarian, energy, mind/body, relationship, centering, east/west, new age, neohealing, integrational, feed-back, balancing, change, self, psychic, reflex, alternative, dimensions, dance, joy, adept, esoteric. All this week, 162279 Highway 1, Big Sur. Call for carpool information.

MONETARY SUCCESS AND FINANCIAL WEALTH ALL DEPEND ON YOUR INCOME. An intensive, 3-day workshop to explore the paths of big money ("megabucks") from the pockets of others into yours. Learn how the more you make, the more you get to keep. Also IRAs and Keogh Plans outlined in a whole-grain atmosphere. The bigger your house and car, the happier you can be. A new principle but an ages-old idea. Be There Then. Merrill, Lynch, Pierce,

Shiva and Vishnu Temple, 6th and Olive, downtown L.A. Call for appt.

FRIDAY

SHARE YOUR INNERMOST FANTASIES WITH US. We will arrange that they can be shared by others, bringing you a new gratification. Write to us now. *Penthouse Forum,* NYC, NY.

THE BLINDING LIGHT BOOKSHOP AND TRAINING CENTER IS HAVING A SALE of used materials all day today. Bargains on candles, mas-sage tables and oils, almost-new astral communicators, Tarot brand household products, pendants and medallions from defunct spiritual avatars and gurus (still useful as Xmas tree decorations), and much much more. Please bring cash.

REALITY IS COMING— ARE YOU READY?

Learn how the unreal is chasing out the real in your own life, and what you can do/not do about it/not it. How

Santa Barbara Maternity Hospital, Main Street, Santa Barbara.

ASTRAL-SMASH—the new video game that lets you fight off the nonbelievers and negatively aligned gremlins as you battle your way to the Higher Plane where Truth, Light, Warmth, and Love await you along with the true knowledge that only cosmic consciousness can bring. Use real quarters or cause quarters to come into your pockets. Now at Play World Arcade, Westwood and Puente Hills Mall.

I AM GOD AND I CAN PROVE IT IF YOU LEND ME YOUR CAR. Today only, please, and I promise to have it back before dark without a scratch, so help Me Me. You know where to reach Me.

SEERS, KEEPERS OF KNOWLEDGES, DEITIES (MAJOR AND MINOR), AVATARS—the William Morris Agency is having an open house today at 1:00 P.M. to inaugurate its new Spiritual Division, catering to your special needs and problems in the areas of contracts, bookings, tax exemptions, publicity, and personal management. Sign up today and we'll only charge 8.5%; after that it's 10%. William Morris Agency, Beverly Hills.

Week 7
SCENES

Y ou are determined to make the Southern California scene, wherever you are. You've accepted the the world's most televised locale. Now is the time to analyze the fine points, to learn that within the Southland there are subscenes, geographic distinctions, and regional specialties. Get out your maps.

Hawaii

This is not a tour guide and we will not cover where to go in Hawaii. What matters here is the *attitude toward* Hawaii. Act as if you might (and do) go there at any moment, on a whim. If someone says he's feeling a bit out of sorts this afternoon, suggest, "Why not go to Hawaii?" Mix drinks for guests according to a recipe you learned at a favorite bar in Hawaii. If possible, drive a car with a Hawaii license plate. Leave messages on your answering machine, "I've gone to Hawaii for the weekend. . . . I'll return your call on Monday. . . . Aloha."

Hawaii is where world-class Southern California tanners go for rays.

The greatest gift one Californian can bestow upon another (apart from giving him space) is to offer the use of one's condominium in Hawaii for the weekend. The greatest gift you can *bring back* from Hawaii is a T-shirt, from a surfing-related business, that is unavailable on the mainland.

Mexico

Wherever you live, the Southern California Anglo will tell you that the Mexican food isn't as good there as it is in Southern California. *Even if you live in Mexico.* The fact is that Southern Californians believe that because of proximity, and because of the blending of cultures and peoples, they have a special franchise on Mexico. But while Southern Californians enjoy travel to spots like Acapulco, Puerto Vallarta, Cancún—the *Love Boat* ports of call—so do people from the rest of the world. It remains for two destinations to be the special province of Southern Californians: Tijuana and Ensenada.

Tijuana has had a long notoriety. Among other things it is still widely believed that there are few acts known to humans, and almost certainly some *not* known, that cannot be witnessed or participated in in Tijuana. For the majority of California visitors to this first town across the border, however, the purpose of the trip is far more prosaic: shopping.

As a Californian you will go to Tijuana when you need more tequila or mezcal, a new cotton blanket for the beach, another pair of *huarache* sandals, or a hooded pullover. If you are under the age of twenty-one, you will hope to get back home with a really dangerous-looking switchblade. Under no circumstances do you want to purchase drugs in Mexico. Why bother, when they're so easy to find back home?

If you go to Tijuana to get *things,* you almost certainly go to Ensenada to get drunk. You will do this at a bar called Hussong's Cantina, whose major intrinsic merit is that everyone else is going there, too. You do not go to Hussong's for a drink or two. You go there for a dozen or two. It is absolutely imperative that you buy a Hussong's bumper sticker if you have a pickup truck or a van. If not, you must buy a Hussong's T-shirt. The reason for this is clear to anyone who has been there even once: if you do Hussong's right, *this memento could be the only way you will remember having been there at all.*

Westwood Village

This neighborhood of shops, restaurants, and theaters adjacent to the UCLA campus is exactly like the main street of any medium-size town in America, except that all the people are rich, young, white, healthy, beautiful, fashionably dressed, well behaved, not

jaywalking, not littering, and on their way to or from a movie.

The thing to do in Westwood is hang out on weekend nights. This is the minidate capital of upscale Los Angeles. The minidate involves a male and a female, fifteen to seventeen years old, dressed in Ralph Lauren's finest, going through the motions of a real adult date. On your minidate you will go to the Westworld amusement arcade to play electronic games until your movie begins, then see the movie, play some more video games, browse in the poster stores, try on some shoes, play some more video. Call home when you're ready for a ride back.

Hollywood and Vine

Despite what the world thinks, Hollywood and Vine is not the crossroads of anything except Hollywood Boulevard and Vine Street. Here is what you will find there:

A bank
A closed department store
A drugstore
A Howard Johnson's

Melrose Avenue

If you're very young and hip and have time and money on your hands on Saturday and Sunday afternoons, there is only one choice for you. You will do Melrose.

Using the used-and-new-and-obsessively-happening clothing store, Flip, as a home base, you will browse through the clothing stores on Melrose Avenue in West Hollywood in order to look around, to buy, and above all, to be seen. This is the spot where last week's idea meets this week's idea. Punks turn into mods. Whatever used-clothing discovery is perceived as the next (or latest) Big Thing is sure to be repeated here in enormous multiples, and the stores are ready to handle it. One day it's four thousand flannel shirts with the sleeves cut off; the next it's fatigue coats with the Who insignia stitched on. Four thousand of them.

The peculiar but endearing Southern California habit of Trying Too Hard—especially in the hipness derby—finds its fullest expression on Melrose, where the avant-garde is a commercial venture and originality can be franchised.

117

Tower Records

If you are in Hollywood at night for any reason whatsoever, you will make a stop at the Tower Records store on the Sunset Strip. Apart from being one of the world's largest record stores, it is a happening scene, a place to be. Perhaps you're in too good a mood to go home with the same old tapes in the car; perhaps you're a rock star eager to see how your latest record is doing; maybe you're just looking for a quick pickup. In any case Tower is open until midnight every day. It takes fifteen minutes to get a space in the parking lot (in Southern California, a sure sign of the worth of a place).

Beverly Hills High School

Beverly Hills may be the only community in the world where it is more fashionable for rich people to send their children to public school than to private school. Why?

The purpose of private school is, of course, so your children won't have to mingle with riffraff. And Beverly Hills has solved that problem very neatly. There *is* no riffraff. Well, no *poor* riffraff, which is what counts.

If you're going to live in Beverly Hills as a student, or if you plan to live in that style anywhere, you must follow these rules.

1. Drive a Rabbit Convertible. Unless, of course, Dad simply insisted on giving you a Porsche.

2. Smoke cigarettes. Marlboros, or clove cigarettes. Girls may smoke lights, or 100's.

3. Make a big fuss over Thai food, about which you are an expert.

4. Have a shrink.

5. Wear thrift-store clothes from Melrose Avenue, or new clothes from Fred Segal. Girls wear Maud Frizon shoes. Boys wear colored Top-Siders.

6. Keep your hair freshly cut and impeccably groomed. For boys, a retroconservative look is appropriate. For girls, nothing too Val-looking.

7. Be bisexual.

8. Forget about pot, except when you need a drug to do on the street. Focus on coke. Learn to judge quality, price, value. Be judgmental about your parents' drugs. Buy mushrooms ('shrooms) for when you see *Quadrophenia*.

9. Have friends whose parents are famous. Use their pool.

10. Have friends who are cute.

Topanga Canyon

Just south of Malibu and running inland from the beach for ten miles or so is a magical place where a man can still wear a ponytail without shame and a woman in a peasant frock is not considered frumpy; where houses may be made from old orange crates and carob is believed to taste good.

Upscale real estate speculation is beginning to tug at the love beads of this charmed community. But for now, those of you looking for a peaceful place where you can walk your goat in town, or a place where the music of the Grateful Dead sounds as fresh as a spring morning, would do well to tune up your old VW bus for a trip up the winding roads of Topanga Canyon.

The Mall

The classic calendar-perfect New England town green, with its white-steepled church and clapboard houses, has its exact social counterpart in the quaint California shopping mall with its three tiers of stores, five tiers of parking, glass elevators, flying escalators, and corn-dog stand. This is the place where the neighborhood gathers to mill about, gossip, socialize, run errands, date, see, and be seen. For the after-school crowd, it's the modern swimmin' hole; for the homemaker, it's the back fence. You dress for the mall, taking note of which mall it is. At the Santa Monica Place mall, jeans and a surf-oriented T-shirt (and no shoes) for males and Dolfin shorts and a pastel sweat shirt for females might be appropriate. At the Sherman Oaks Galleria, this week's full Val treatment is de rigueur. At the Malibu Country Mart (an outdoor shopping complex, not a mall really) a sweat suit and a watch worth over seventy-five hundred dollars make the most sense. At the Beverly Center in West Hollywood (not so much a mall as a nation), wear a compass so that *just in case* you should ever want to leave, you can find your car.

Unlike in the rest of the country, in Southern California it is perfectly acceptable to take your meals in a mall restaurant.

The Valley

Until 1982, when aided by Frank and Moon Zappa's song "Valley Girl" it discovered a new pride, the San Fernando Valley (which from now on you will only call "The Valley") enjoyed a reputation as the New Jersey of Southern California. A more-than-necessary suburb of Los Angeles, from which it is just across the Santa Monica Mountains (from now on, "over the hill"), it was accused by the cruel L.A. sophisticates of being a giant, soulless, ugly sprawl of expensive but rinky-dink suburbia—a haven of materialistic and conformist values.

Well, now we know the truth. It is all those things. And we think that's wonderful. We show how wonderful by saying things like:

1. "There really are some nice parts to the Valley." This is never uttered sarcastically, only patronizingly. When pressed for an example, mention something about "some nice horse country around Calabasas."

2. "It's way out in the Valley." If you are a non-Val, you will always imagine the Valley to be in the farthest reaches of the desert, even though it begins just a few minutes from the Sunset Strip. You should complain about and dread a trip to the Valley.

3. "No Vals Allowed," "Vals Go Home," "Death to Vals." If you are a surfer who lives in a beach town, the Val surfer is your sworn enemy. Waves are, after all, a limited natural resource, and Vals are the stripminers of the swells. As a gesture of civic pride, you are expected to cause bodily harm to any Vals attempting to usurp your God-given surf spots or—at the very least—to be as rude as possible to them.

4. "She's a Val."
This means one of two things:
A. She's a tease; she's hard to get.
B. She's easy.

5. "They live in the Valley but south of the freeway." This means they're okay—the better (read *richer*) parts of the Valley are generally found on the south side of the Ventura Freeway, which splits the Valley into two parts.

The Desert

When you live someplace where the weather is always temperate, the sun always shines, and there are more recreational opportunities than in the rest of the world put together, what do you do to get away from it all?

You go someplace swelter-ing, where it gets dark in the middle of the afternoon and where there is *nothing whatso-ever to do.* Palm Springs and its neighboring towns. And don't argue that there's plenty of golf and tennis and sunbathing in Palm Springs, because there's no dearth of that anywhere in the Southland. The correct thing to do in Palm Springs is nothing. You should do this all day (which does not preclude reading a few scripts, or drinking a few tall cool ones) until at last it is fully evening and you can get in your car and go to a really big restaurant and wait in line for a table.

For your sojourn in The Desert (which is what you must call Palm Springs) you will need the following:

1. Platinum hair, teased *big* (Women only)
2. Loud golf pants with coordinated shirt (Men only)
3. An electric golf cart to prevent accidental exercise
4. A really big Cadillac, preferably in a silvery-blue color
5. A P.S. I LOVE YOU bumper sticker (P.S. = Palm Springs)

The intersection of Bob Hope Drive and Frank Sinatra Drive will be found in The Desert, which should tell you all you need to know.

North vs. South

The correct attitude for Bay Area residents toward Southern California is that they hate the place, and go there as infrequently as possible. Southern California is, after all, hedonistic and plastic.

The correct attitude for Southern Californians toward the Bay Area is that it's a great place, a lot of fun, charming, and one should try to go there as often as possible. They are skeptical only toward Marin County, because natives still prefer redwood hot tubs to concrete spas.

W vs. E

Southern Californians have set perceptions of the East Coast defined alternately as Everything Other Than Southern California, or as New York City. These perceptions are entirely rooted in fact—in the fact, that is, that it is impossible for a Southern Californian to conceive of any enjoyable or rewarding life outside of Southern California. Here are your new attitudes toward the East:

1. "Everybody's so *hyper* in the East." This can be proved by any show of enthusiasm or vitality on the part of someone known to be from the East. The same behavior in a westerner is something else. It is "being stoked," "going for it," or "hot," which is far more conducive to a life free of stress, worry, or hypertension.

2. "How can you stand the winters?" The ability and inclination to survive the changing seasons in the East is not to be seen as a building block of sturdy character, but as a sign of lunacy or, at best, as grounds for pity.

3. "New York (or Boston, or Chicago, or Washington, et cetera) must be so *exciting*! So much to *do*! So much *culture*!" (The part about "... but I can't for the life of me imagine why anyone would want to live there" is silently understood.) These phrases are uttered as a way of making visitors feel a little less awkward about not being tanned. Please consider exactly how sincere this will sound coming from between a set of perfect white teeth, set into a magnificently bronzed face on a remarkably fit body.

4. "Where is that?"
Southern Californians have no idea where the following places are: Rhode Island, Bloomingdale's, Bermuda, the basement.

Week 8
PEOPLE

Because California is a state which people seem to come to far more often than from, it is a catchall of more different types of people than almost anywhere else. Since you couldn't possibly hope to be like all of them, this week we're going to concentrate on those types whom by now you've come to feel you ought to be like. These are the people whom you have seen living the good life in the best made-for-TV sense of the phrase.

The California Girl

Yes, the California Girl is real. She exists. That's right—*just like in the orange soda ads.*

She can be found all over Southern California, but espe-

cially at the beach. As you have probably already surmised, she is fair of hair (long, colored by the sun) and fair of form (long, colored by the sun).

What you may be surprised to learn is that she is *not* full of herself or snotty. Rather, she is relentlessly cheerful. She says "Hi!" and smiles. A whole lot. She has great teeth.

Is she an airhead? Many people have asked. The correct answer is, *not necessarily.* She simply doesn't feel the need to wear her intellect on her sleeve. In fact, she rarely wears sleeves.

What she does wear is wrap shorts. Or Dolfin shorts. A string bikini. A white gauze dress. Levi's. Perfect Levi's. And when it gets cold?

This is California. It doesn't.

The California Girl is into the beach, dance exercise, her car, having a good time, and being happy.

Is that one-dimensional? Maybe. So?

Aggressively Laid Back

This person has embraced the relaxed, mellow Southern California life with a vengeance. The aggressively laid-back guy—or A L B—is always on edge, making sure that nothing unmellow passes his way. His favorite phrase is "Mellow out" (more accurately, *"Mellow out, man!"*) and he perpetually pities all those uncool people who are still hyper. He loves to lie out in the sun but he is jangling his car keys the whole time. For some reason he tends to have a beard, be slightly balding, be very darkly tanned, drive an Alfa-Romeo Spider, work in The Industry, and talk loudly about it in restaurants, and carry a cigarette case containing at least half a dozen perfectly rolled joints.

The Ex-New Yorker

The ex-New Yorker's single greatest source of pride is that he or she had the incredible wisdom and good fortune to leave New York City for these sunnier shores. The ex-NYer is so proud that he sports a vanity license plate which says X NY or NY TO LA or some such. He likes California even better than the natives, wishes he were a native, and considers all the years before his move wasted.

Still, he sneaks a peek at the Sunday *New York Times* every week, uses alien phrases like "standing *on* line," and "chop meat" as a noun, and says that one thing he misses is egg creams. Egg creams and hot dog vendors. Oh, and night life. Yeah, and Checker cabs. . . .

Dry-Cleaned Punk

In California, punk is not dead. But it's different from punk in its heyday in New York and London. California punk is squeaky clean. It is never threatening. It never involves mutilating any part of the body in any way that could not occur in an ear-piercing clinic at the shopping mall, except for the odd tattoo. California punk is black sleeveless T-shirts with sophisticated graphics. California punk is humorous hair. California punk grows not out of urban squalor but out of suburban trend-setting. And following. It's not about anger; it's about shopping.

For a while California *did* continue the tradition of punk music very successfully, of which surf punk may well have been the cutting edge. Only in California could you hear the raw sounds of East Village subbasement clubs played in Hollywood night spots where blond surfers in Sex Wax T-shirts slam-danced with Beverly Hills sweet-sixteeners in dry-cleaned microminis charged to Daddy's last TV pilot.

But since the dawning of the rock video age, that cutting edge has dulled somewhat, making way for the advent of Mods.

Vals

Myth: A Valley Girl is just a WASP acting like a Jewish American Princess.

Truth: There are Jewish Valley Girls.

The Stoner

The Stoner would be in high school, if he ever went. He is more frequently found, however, at the side of the road, staring dumbfounded at his car, which is somehow not running. He wears a black T-shirt with a pseudodisturbing image and the logo of a heavy metal band. His characteristic saying is "What?"

The Stoner carries a big comb or brush (he is one of the few males left with long hair). In the end he doesn't get the girl.

The Leftover Hippie

The Leftover Hippie lives in Topanga Canyon, in a house made from old orange crates. Time and economics have made the home worth somewhere in the mid-six figures. The LH will still travel to the Bay Area by Volkswagen at the drop of a hat to catch a Grateful Dead concert, but will just as readily travel to Merrill Lynch to discuss an investment portfolio. The LH no longer believes in LSD, but still believes in astrology and in organic foods. He keeps a goat at home.

The LH's children are heavily into computers, and this worries him a whole lot.

How to Appear Rich

Here is one of the most important skills you can master. And you don't have to be poor to reap its benefits. *It is just as important to appear rich if you* are *rich as it is if you are not.* The rich person who pretends otherwise is shamefully squandering his talents.

Since the biggest expense for the Southern California rich is usually the home, if you can't afford something in seven figures, start doing everything away from your home. Meet people for lunch in restaurants. Suggest doing things at *their* houses. Offer to pick them up, or to meet them wherever you're going.

And since the next biggest expense is your car, learn how to rent. *Any* car can be rented in Southern California, and if you are clever you will have a standing arrangement with Budget Rent-A-Car in Beverly Hills (remember that

name) always to be given the same car. And of course when the car is rented, you can be that much more casual in blithely tossing your keys to the valet parking attendant.

Next, learn how to *accessorize*. Certain items are available to *anyone* who isn't too intimidated to shop on Rodeo Drive. The classics in this category are, of course, the Gucci key chain (the bigger the gold "G"s, the better) and the Louis Vuitton signature credit card holder. Even if you have no credit cards. Both accessories are affordable and suggest that you have lots more in those lines at home.

In the upscale communities, an expensive haircut is absolutely crucial, and is always worth the investment. You must be able to say, for example, not just that you go to Gene's, but that you go to *Gene* at Gene's.

Since your watch tells a lot more about you than just what time it is, if you can't afford the solid gold Rolex, you might as well kill yourself. If this is not within your means, you *could* consider a stainless-and-gold Rolex, an all-stainless, a Cartier Santos, or a Porsche Designs black watch. If even *this* is beyond you, Seiko makes a pretty slick copy of the gold Rolex at a reasonable price. *But . . .* since the Gold Rolex is the subject of so much surreptitious scrutiny to determine authenticity, you might feel less conspicuous with the Seiko version of the gold-and-stainless version of the Rolex. Got it?

If you can afford a house, but not in, say, Beverly Hills, you might start looking at the many real estate listings that advertise "BHPO" in them, which means Beverly Hills Post Office. These houses tend to cost somewhat less than those in Beverly Hills proper, and while they do not grant you the Beverly Hills city services (which are legendary), they *do* allow you to get your mail through the Beverly Hills Post Office, which means a *very desirable return address on your mail*.

Since clothes are tough to manage on a tight budget, take your cue from the *real* rich people who make a trademark of always wearing a warmup suit. Lay out enough cash for one overpriced Fila outfit (a lot of polyester, a lot of money, but a lot of clout) and wear it everywhere, on the principle that only the rich can afford to look casual *all* the time.

Tip big. If you think you can't afford it, then order cheaper. But tip big and wave that tip around.

And finally, remember a tiny, tiny dab of excess baby powder just above the upper lip.

California Classics

Face it—we all know some people who are more California than others. And when those people are in the public eye, they deserve special recognition because they serve as role models, as ambassadors, or as mascots of Southern California.

Just as surely as Woody Allen, William F. Buckley, and Jean Harris are *not* Southern California, so these special few would never have been what they are without Southern California. As a special award, these people are hereby dubbed California Classics.

FARRAH

Because she is blond; because she is the role model for thousands of women in Marina Del Rey; because she is blond; because grown men wept when she left a TV series; because she is blond; because she can get a table at Spago; because she is the preeminent practitioner of the California state gesture, the smile; and finally because not only does she happen to be blond, she is the very *definition* of blond—ask anyone.

HOBIE

Because he was born a surfer and went on to revolutionize the surfboard; because he knows the difference between recreation and commerce and deliberately blurs the distinction in his own life; because he owns no coat and tie; because he invented the Hobie Cat catamaran; because his wife is named Kahala; because he still makes surfboards, purely for pleasure.

JOAN

Because she has become the Beverly Hills lady par excellence; because she can talk about tummy tucks and fanny lifts as casually as other people talk about the weather; because she says "Gucci" better than anyone else; because she named her daughter Melissa; because she helps out Johnny; and because she knows that the size of your ring matters, and that it matters a whole lot.

JOHNNY

Because the first question asked of any other California Classic is always "What's Johnny *really* like?"; because his was the only home that carried the warning on the Map of the Stars' Homes, *Do Not Loiter!;* because his image as the ultimate midwesterner could exist only in contrast to its Southern California context; because of tennis; because he is impressed with Carl Sagan's intellect; and because Bob Hope drops in unexpectedly.

MERV

Because he is the highest clearing house for all Southern California personalities; because he is called, simply, *Merv;* because he wants to know have you been to

Rodeo Drive yet? And have you seen the *prices*?; because he appreciates the Gabors; because he knows that tennis is a fit conversational topic for any occasion; because "doing Merv" is one of the sacraments of Hollywood publicity; and because if Southern California didn't exist, Merv would have invented it.

JON

Because Jon Peters is the Hair Stylist to the Star; because he used to be the Hair Stylist to the Stars; because he proves that anyone can grow up to become a producer; because he can see Streisand whenever he wants; because he has two first names.

SAMMY

Because Vegas is, after all, a function of Southern California; because he is a close, close, personal, personal, friend, friend; because he bought the first of the Gucci Edition of the Cadillac Seville; because he defines the gold standard; because he weathered being mentioned in Linda Lovelace's autobiography; and because anyone who hugs Nixon will hug *anybody,* and *that's* California.

Week 9

SEX

***H**ow to Get Members of the Opposite Sex to Smile at You in California? Smile at them. Their responses will be automatic. Californians are the smiliest people in America.*

How Californians Find Partners

THE STOPLIGHT PICKUP

Probably the most popular and most original of all pickups in Southern California. You pull up to a stoplight in your car. Someone pulls up next to you. You make the traditional eye contact. A potential partner? Well, you already know quite a bit about her. You know what she drives (see Week 1, "Cars") and if you were observant you may have noticed from her license-plate frame a crucial fact—where she's from, what sport she likes, marital status ("Happiness Is Being Single"), age ("Happiness Is Being a Grandparent"), or, from a vanity license plate, her name. With a little experience you can judge her height.

Perhaps you can hear what radio station she's listening to, or, if her windows are closed, you may be able to tell the station by searching for one on your own radio that matches the beat to which she is grooving. In either case, indicate that you are listening to the same station.

If it isn't already open, open your window. Wait for the potential partner to open her window, too. Perhaps you will have to use the international symbol for "Please open your window": a hand cranking air. (The symbol is used even for electric windows.)

Say hi. Try some oblique opening line, like "Wanna go out for lunch?" If it's not mealtime or cocktail hour, you can also suggest "I'm going to the do-it-yourself car wash. Wanna go, too?" If the answer is yes, just say "follow me" and you're all set. (Incidentally, the car wash happens to be a hell of a romantic spot.) Once you get really good at this kind of pickup, you can try, as a final fillip, "How about we just skip lunch" (or "Shouldn't we change before we wash the cars?").

THE GROUP STOPLIGHT PICKUP

Especially popular with the youth of Beverly Hills and certain beach towns, it works like this. A group of cute teen-age girls in a VW Scirocco pull up next to a group of cute teen-age guys in a Jeep. After much good-natured hooting, snickering, and elbows in the ribs, a plan is made to meet at a party—always a safe spot for further investigation of the other group. The light turns green. There is a drag race for a couple of blocks. The cars go their separate ways, and in each car there is a little argument about who gets whom.

TRAFFIC SCHOOL PICKUP

Traffic school is a pretty good place to meet partners, since people there usually share your interests.

THE SUPERMARKET PICKUP

A special case must be made here for the Boys Market (the name is corporate and does not refer to the clientele) in Marina Del Rey, which, it is safe to say, is the swingles capital of what is already the swingles capital of the swingles capital of America. There the most eligible singles in all of Southern California parade up and down the aisles, picking up a can of Campbell's soup here, a Stouffer's frozen entrée there, but shopping for much, much more. The best time is about six to eight P.M., the best departments are deli and, especially, fruits and vege-tables—a Garden of Eden setting replete with apples. Here, the trick is to play dumb. Wait for a likely prospect. Pick up something, anything—an onion, a coconut, it doesn't matter—and when the prospect passes, say, "Excuse me, but do you know how to cook this?" With any luck you will soon be enjoying a home cooking lesson. Incidentally, shopping carts in Southern California are designed so that all four wheels swivel (not just the front two), which makes it surprisingly easy to lose control and accidentally bump into someone cute.

THE JOGGING PICKUP

On the jogging path, however, you must never bump into anyone, or you'll kill your chances right there. The jogging path gives you a chance to judge the body and general physical conditioning of prospects. The state-of-the-art swingles jogging path is San Vicente Boulevard in Brentwood, on the grassy tree-lined mall down the center of the street. Here, only serious, regular runners make real headway. You will want to be in top form for this marathon. Buy (and break in, please) top-of-the-line New Balance running shoes. Go for your run at the same time every day. Remember—these are serious young professionals, so don't even try during office hours. The idea is to notice someone for a while. Be cool—just a little con-centrating-too-hard-to-pause nod, not too broad a smile—at first. When you are ready to make your move, you might try running alongside your pros-pect for a while. When this involves your having to change directions to join her (or him), you have just made the most romantic gesture possible toward a runner, and your chances of finishing the race are very, very good.

SINGLES ENCOUNTERS

Various spiritual and "wholistic" retreats offer singles encounter weekends and evenings, generally billed as an opportunity for adult singles to get together in a warm, loving, nude, nonsexual setting with hot tubs and private relaxation rooms. It is a chance to shed any negative or mixed feelings that might have poisoned your mind regarding the concept of meeting perfect strangers stark naked, sharing a hot tub or a massage, and then *only perhaps* (always "only perhaps") having hot, animal sex and never seeing them again.

THE AIRPLANE PICKUP

Southern Californians, accustomed to long-distance travel, are perfectly at home on East Coast–West Coast flights, and can perform most of their usual daily functions in the air.

Meditating, jogging, writing screenplays, taking meetings—all are done regularly in 747's. And so are pickups. The prime airline is American, the best flights are the "red eye" ten P.M. flight from LAX to JFK in New York, and the noon flight from JFK to LAX. The best section for pickups used to be first class, but this tends now to be a forum for making high-powered business contacts, and the real singles scene (including peo-ple who are singles only when in the air) is in the tourist section. Freed from ordinary earthly restraints, the Southern Californian enjoys taking chances aloft. When those chances are actually consummated aloft (generally in the lavatory, though on late-night flights a blanket provides some privacy), the participants become members of the "Mile High Club," the subject of more locker-room boasting than tennis prowess and business acumen combined.

NATURE SEX

The balmy climate of Southern California makes sex in the wilds possible and popular. You should think of it as a way of being at one (or two, or more, depending) with the plants and animals and sun and rocks and sharp sticks and insects. Sure, Nature Sex is a bit sixties, but that's cool in California. It also overlaps with an area known as Sex for Display Purposes, which is only slightly less cool.

BUSINESS SEX

If you have used sex to advance yourself in The Industry, or in any other Southern California business setting, you must learn not to feel guilty. Discovering that both sides of a business arrangement are interested in sex is just a way of forming a common bond, like finding out that the other person likes golf or sushi. And if you cause or run into a situation where sexual pressure is exerted in a business setting, you are on the wrong track. Sex in business should be just a getting-to-know-you kind of thing. Taking a meeting or taking a quickie, it's all the same thing—just another way for two people in business to stroke each other.

Sex at the Beach

Sex at the beach is one of the prerequisites of life in Southern California. This does not mean actually *doing it* right there in the sand—that would be in bad taste, even in Southern California. Beach sex is more of a mating dance, with a few steps of water ballet thrown in.

PREPARING FOR THE BEACH

You must not go to the beach without a tan. After all, you will be exposing a considerable expanse of your flesh. Now, you probably thought that the point of going to the beach was to *get* that tan. Well, you were wrong. The point of going is to display your tan. Then, how do you get your tan? The answer is the same as that given by the Bostonian woman asked where she got her hats: "We don't get them, we have them."

Okay, okay. There is a secret that you might as well know. Go to the beach *midweek* at first, until your tan is at the

weekend-maintenance stage.

DO YOU GO INTO THE WATER OR NOT?

It depends. Have you ever seen what you look like wet?

LOTION

Never turn down a request from a Potential Partner (PP) to help her or him with suntan lotion. Deftly applied to the back and thighs, Hawaiian Tropic has distinct aphrodisiac properties. And if the request involves an oil-base preparation, your weekend plans are settled.

APPROACHING SOME-ONE AT THE BEACH

Do not walk directly up to a Potential Partner and start a conversation. Common courtesy dictates that you use a ploy, or ruse, as an icebreaker. Typically, your Frisbee goes out of control onto someone's blanket. Dogs can be trained to run to the "wrong" master on silent command, necessitating retrieval. It is most proper to jog past the PP once or twice, affording you both adequate check-out time. Don't run *too* close, however, or you could cause sand to be kicked toward the PP.

SOME IMPORTANT RULES

Women: do not distract a surfer watching for waves. **Men:** do not distract a woman watching for surfers.

THE HOT TUB SPA

The hot tub spa used to be a motel. But times changed. Out went the beds. In came the Jacuzzis, the diagonal wood paneling, the hanging plants. Maybe a massage table. Soft lights. Soft music. Presto—suddenly the sleaze has gone out of renting rooms by the hour.

The hot tub spa is the ideal alternative to the your-place-or-mine quandary. Remember to make the reservation *before* you go out on that date. Just in case.

NUDITY AND THE SOCIAL JACUZZI

If you're visiting someone in a nonsexual setting and everyone goes into the Jacuzzi naked, will you have to take off your clothes, too? Well, you *could* wear a swimsuit, but that would call attention to the whole issue, thus sexualizing the nonsexual setting. Nudity in the Jacuzzi should *not* be construed as necessarily erotic; it is more often a purely family activity.

RECREATIONAL SEX

Sex that is particularly successful, unfettered by commitment, and generally energetic is highly regarded in Southern California, where it is known as Good Recreational Sex. (There is no such thing as Bad Recreational Sex. Bad sex, however strenuous, is considered poor exercise.)

Recreational Sex is something that you should have every once in a while, or at any rate not more than eight or ten times in a weekend. Beyond that point it becomes professional, or marathon, sex. Marathon Sex is run on a 26.2 mile course through Marina Del Rey.

The requirements for participating in Recreational are not as stringent as many people think. A partner is generally necessary, and you may be called upon to identify your sign of the zodiac before engaging in sexual activity.

DIVORCE

Californians may become depressed following divorce, but more likely they will be quick to reassure you, "Oh, don't worry; we're both much happier. Better friends than we ever were. We planned it this way from the beginning."

In either case it is customary to throw a party. Address books make nice gifts.

Week 10

THE INDUSTRY

*I*f you have to ask what is meant by "The Industry," you'll never have a pay-or-play, three-picture deal.

The Industry refers to anything remotely connected with entertainment, based on the common belief that Los Angeles is a company town with only one kind of business. If you work in the movies, radio, TV, music—you are in The Industry. If you are a president of Paramount Pictures and/or if you work in a Fotomat, you're in The Industry.

Surrounding The Industry there are the Sort-of Jobs. These allow you to answer the perennial question "Are you in The Industry?" with the second most common answer, "Sort of." (The most common answer in Southern California is, of course, "Yes.") "Sort of," if you baby-sit for a movie star's kids, cut a record producer's hair, or repair a news commentator's car.

There is a companion answer to "Sort of," which is "No, but most of my friends are."

Power in The Industry

Power in The Industry is a Byzantine structure, made more complicated by its constant shifting from day to day. Nonetheless, understanding the order of power is absolutely crucial to your success. Here is a sample—a diagram of the chain of command in one recent week.

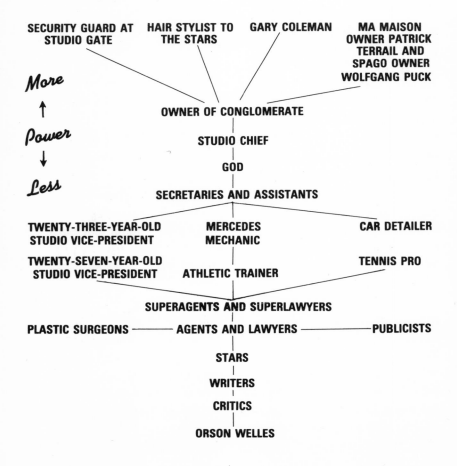

The Industry Office

When is an office not an office?

If you are in The Industry, or if you want to seem to be, it will be necessary to make your office as *unlike* an office as possible. The Industry executive's office has no desk. A dining-room table, a Parsons table, a giant black glass coffee table—any of these may be present, but nothing that could possibly appear to hold pencils, files, paper clips, or rubber bands.

All files, papers, supplies, reference books, and the rest of the ordinary paraphernalia of office work are maintained by your secretary (or, if you are an agent, your assistant) in a separate room. (Except for a tall pile of scripts, which you can point to whenever you need to pretend to be too busy to do something you don't want to do.) Your assistant is also official beverage host, and maintains the compact refrigerator which you must have in the anteroom. It should be stocked with Coca-Cola, apple juice in cans, orange juice in cans, Perrier water (remember to have an opener on hand), and Tab. *Especially Tab.* All guests must be offered something from the fridge before they enter your office, even if they're rushing in to tell you that a brush fire is racing toward your house.

There must also be a couch in your office—ideally, two couches forming an L. Large end tables and a massive coffee table help. You should give the impression that you could, if you wished, perform psychoanalysis at any moment.

You will have two telephones in your office, of the multiline variety. One phone is on your nondesk, one is at the end of the couch. A sure sign of power is when you have a phone at *each* end of the couch. During any given meeting there will be a moment when at least three phone calls are happening in

the same room, some on hold.

If on the East Coast every office of any stature has a framed photograph of the occupant shaking hands with a politician, in The Industry office there must be photographs of stars. Movie, recording, whatever—all that matters is that you appear with the star in the photograph. (If you don't have such a photograph, seek the services of a good airbrush artist.) Photographs of just stars alone make your office look like a delicatessen.

The art on your walls is crucial. If you are in The Music Industry, a few simple gold or platinum records, framed, make their own quiet statement. In TV a Nielsen box nailed to the wall with a

spike is a cute touch, and in The Film Industry posters are the thing—posters from successful movies that feature your name prominently in the credits. If no such posters exist, buy an assortment of posters from one single blockbuster movie. With enough of them on display, guests will just naturally assume that you had something important to do with the project, and they will be afraid to show their ignorance by inquiring just what it was.

Electronic accessories should include a videocassette recorder and TV, an expensive stereo system (especially for you music types) and some kind of toy. A video game perhaps, or a computer, or a high-tech computerized exercise bicycle.

If your office is actually in L.A., you should have some art by a leading Los Angeles artist such as Chuck Arnoldi, Ed Moses, Ed Ruscha, Billy Al Bengston, or David Hockney. There is a bonus if the art depicts property owned by you, or persons related to you. Extra bonus if it *is* you.

Items from the Studio Gift Shop

SCRIPT COVER/REFLECTORS

These script covers, printed with your choice of agency and studio logos, have no pages inside, but their inner surfaces are mirrored, allowing you to improve your tan and still look busy at the beach. Handy for magazines, too.

PREWRITTEN MEMO PADS

Memos from all the right people. Leave these scattered across your desk—look important. Or, send them out—confound your colleagues! Spielberg memos slightly more expensive.

QUICK-CHANGE POSTER SETS

Remember those pull-down maps in geography class? The same system has been adapted for movie posters. Make visiting stars, directors, producers feel at home when they see *their* ad on *your* wall. In racks of four, six, and for publicity departments, twelve.

WRITERS' T-SHIRTS

Nip that annoying question in the bud. These hundred-percent cotton T-shirts are screen-printed with the message NO, I'M *NOT* WORKING ON A SCREENPLAY. White on black or black on white.

FALSE BIRTH CERTIFICATES

In sets of four, each one more recent than the last. Shed unwanted years! Become a baby mogul overnight.

INFLATABLE CASTING COUCH

For smaller offices.

PRERECORDED INCOMING MESSAGE CASSETTES

Wait until all your dinner guests have arrived, then say that you forgot to listen to your messages, and switch on this cassette. Watch their respect for you grow when they hear what Warren, Jack, Sherry, Swifty, and others have to say.

PORTABLE PARKING SPACE

Made from flexible asphalt sheeting. Looks just like an ordinary parking space but it rolls up for stowing neatly in your trunk. Just lay it down over an existing space and pull right in. Never be late for another meeting! Allow about four weeks for printing with your name.

ASHTRAYS, TOWELS, AND BATHROBES FROM THE BEST HOTELS

Avoid the embarrassment and nuisance of snitching them.

HYDRAULIC CHAIR LIFTER

Actually grow taller during meetings! Intimidating as hell.

INFLATABLE *YOU*

Bring it to screenings and leave early. A real timesaver. Deluxe model includes cassettes for realistic responses to comedies, thrillers, romances.

BICOASTAL NECKTIE

Reverses to gold chain. Stylish, convenient.

The Coast Calling

Okay—the crew from the phone company has just left and it's time to get down to business. People in The Industry like using the phone because it's so much more *personal* than a face-to-face meeting. After all, when you meet in person, everyone's always on the phone to somewhere else and it's hard to get their attention.

So, let's say you want to

call someone. Your mother, perhaps. Pick up the phone. Buzz your secretary and tell him or her what you want this way: "Get my mother." Hang up. The secretary will now call your mother and tell her, "(Your name) calling for Mother."

If your mother is used to Industry calls, she will have discerned that it is not actually you but your secretary, and will answer, "Okay," and wait. If your mother is a complete hayseed she may begin talking to your secretary thinking it's you. Don't worry. Mom will learn.

Now your secretary will buzz back to you. "I have your mother now." Thank the secretary. Count to twenty (thirty, if you're having a fight with your mother) and pick up the line. "Hi, Mom?"

As you should have guessed by now, this exercise isn't about saving time, it's about exercising power. If you want to wield power *back* when you get that call, "Hello, please hold for Mike Mogul," pretend to be finishing up a conversation when Mike Mogul gets on the line: "... just tell Barbra if she doesn't sing 'People' at the kid's Bar

153

Mitzvah there's no deal yeah Hi Mike what were you calling about?"

When and where to receive phone calls is an art, too, in The Industry. In addition to taking as many calls as possible during meetings, you will want to receive calls in public places, in particular the Polo Lounge at the Beverly Hills Hotel and the pool at the Beverly Hills Hotel. At both of these places your name will be announced quite loudly and distinctly for everyone to hear. Of course by now being paged at the Beverly Hills has become such an Industry cliché (and it is so widely believed that anyone who is paged has arranged it in advance with his or her secretary) that you may want to give some consideration to the distinction of *not* being paged, but instead, having a discreet note passed to your table or lounge chair. In full view of everyone else, of course.

The second best way to exercise power over the phone is through the Box. The Box is the speaker phone and it's annoying as hell to the other party, which can be quite useful. The beginning and end of each bit of conversation get lopped off, your voice sounds remote, and you come across very, very powerful. If you really want to go on record as doing a favor for someone, start a conversation on the Box and after a few moments say, "Hang on a second—I'm gonna switch this damn thing off." If you want to get back at someone who is using the Box, attack the quality of his equipment: "It sounds like you're talking from the bottom of a *garbage can*!" (Incidentally, it is *never done* to use the Box on anyone who wields true power over you. Nobody calls Marvin Davis, who owns 20th Century-Fox, on the Box. Nobody sane, that is.)

It is also imperative that you have an answering machine or service. With a machine, you are under some obligation to program it with a message that is either mercifully short or extremely clever. The sin here is being boring. If you opt for the clever approach, beware. It becomes necessary to change messages frequently, or callers start complaining, "I already *heard* that one." Incidentally, people still really do say, "Have your machine call my machine," but it never sounds very fresh or funny.

When you receive a particularly choice, impressive message—from, say, Ray Stark, or Victoria Principal—save it, and in the middle of a dinner party say, "Good heavens, I forgot to listen to my machine!" Then play it back for the assembled guests. Remember not to play the same message twice to the same guests.

To avoid all this trouble, there are answering services that are generally staffed by aspiring Industry types. Especially actors. They will, without charging extra and

THREE TELEPHONE PROBLEMS

1. You are having a phone conversation when there is a "click" on the line. The person with whom you are conversing says, "Was that yours or mine?" What does that mean?

2. Someone asks you, "Why didn't you call? Didn't you get my message?" What do you say?

3. Someone tells you, "I tried to get you all week but there was no answer." You suspect him of lying. What do you do?

ANSWERS

1. He has call-waiting, and another call has come through. If you want to pretend you have it, too, you could quietly disconnect the call, then call back later to apologize: "My call-waiting screwed up."

2. You say, "Oh, my answering service always screws up. You know—aspiring actors." Roll your eyes.

3. Answer, "I have a service."

without being asked, provide commentary on the messages they have taken down for you. "Sherry Lansing called about that deal but I happen to know that it's going to fall through. Mike Mogul called to say he can't make it to lunch because he's sick but just between us we handle his messages and he's actually having lunch at Musso's with some agent—do you want me to find out who?"

And of course you will need to have a phone in your car. If you can't afford one, just take a phone from your house with you when you drive and hold the receiver up, which looks pretty good to everyone but truck drivers and bus passengers. You might also try making calls from a pay phone near a busy street and saying, "I can't hear you too well, I'm calling from the middle of traffic," which sounds great until the operator tells you to deposit another quarter.

Finally, agents have a special relationship with the telephone. It's where they live. If you can get your agent on the phone on the first try, look for another agent. If your agent calls you, be sure to have a magazine on hand to pass the time during the periods you are put on hold. Please try to be understanding about this trait in your agent. Remember, your agent is just like you, from the wrist up.

From the wrist down, he is Bell System property.

How to Take a Meeting

As you probably know by now, you do not give a meeting, hold a meeting, attend a meeting, or go to a meeting. That's for the PTA. You can only *take a meeting*.

Actually, if an idea (or in The Industry, "concept") is strong enough to warrant further discussion after an initial feeler, you *can* "go to meeting" with it, which simply means you will make plans to take a meeting soon.

"Take" is both active and passive, in the sense that it refers to the person in whose office the meeting occurs, as well as the people who come from elsewhere.

Once a meeting has been set up, you must check with the others planning to attend to see if anyone needs a ride over there. No one will accept, and you should not accept anyone else's offer. Everyone must drive him- or herself to the meeting. If the meeting is on a studio lot, or other limited-access complex, you will be sure to ask the secretary of the meeting-planner (but never the meeting-planner directly) for a "drive-on"—the pass which allows you to take your car onto the studio lot (lot refers to the studio campus here, *not* the parking lot). This pass will be waiting for you at the gate. If it isn't there—even if you know full well that it isn't there because you're not supposed to have one—*make a big fuss*. Repeat who you are to the guard and say, "I can't understand why; there was supposed to be one waiting for me. Please check again." The guard will check again, and then will suggest that you call whoever you're seeing, on the house phone in that little booth over there. It is a measure of your sense of power if you can persuade the guard to make the call for you. Once the pass is arranged, the guard's manner will change abruptly from surly to fawning, and he will say, "You may go ahead. Do you know where that office is?"

Even if you have no idea where that office is, say "Sure." You must not appear unfamiliar with the studio. The guard will tell you where you may park—in the visitors' lot—and you will listen only halfheartedly, then go ahead and park wherever you wish, except in a space reserved for someone more powerful than yourself. The rape of a parking space is not easily forgiven in The Industry.

Once you get to the correct office (a little late, please— don't appear too eager), expect to be kept waiting until everyone due at the meeting has arrived. The secretary will offer you a drink, which you will accept. Do not ask for an alcoholic beverage. Ask for a Perrier, apple juice, tomato juice, or Tab. Be courteous when the secretary asks you if you would ever

be interested in looking over a script that he or she wrote. *Say yes.* As in most industries, secretaries have the power to break you, if not make you.

As soon as everyone is present, interrupt the meeting just as it is starting, to call your own office. Ask if there are any messages. If you want to impress people, you might ask if specific people called. Jack? Warren? Meryl? Tell your secretary where you are and what the number is, then say, "Don't put any calls through unless they're urgent." You should have arranged with your secretary to put *all* calls through. Ask your host if you can make just one more call. Call Rome.

Then the meeting will begin. After a minute the host will say, "Hold on just a second. We should be taking this down." A search for a stenographer will ensue. Now is your chance to get back on the phone.

At regular intervals some- one should interrupt the meet- ing to ask an unrelated question. Does anyone know a good BMW mechanic? Has anyone here ever been to Bora

Bora? This helps to regulate the flow of the ideas.

If the meeting runs long, you will want to get up and pace around a little bit. If you do this right, it should afford you a good view of the documents on your host's desk. (If you are the host, you should have arranged in advance of the meeting, on your desk, information you want leaked.)

The host will end the meeting abruptly by saying

he has to drive to the tennis shop before it closes to pick up his rackets, which are being restrung. "Can I drop you somewhere?"

Answer: "No, I have the Porsche here." The host will say, "Then let me walk you to it." At your car the host will compliment you on it. Then he will turn around and get into his own, better car. Or, if his car is less impressive than yours, he will simply wave good-bye.

How The Industry Works

Hollywood is a collection of creative businesses near (but rarely in) the area of Los Angeles known as Hollywood. The principal creative product of Hollywood is the *deal*. The deal is an agreement arrived at in a series of *meetings*

wherein a group of business-men agree to continue doing business together, principally at more meetings. In the *motion picture* end of The Industry, *movies* are occasionally made as a sort of sideline to the deal. These movies are known as *product*. In the television end of The Industry, when the deals go on long enough, they may go on to the next stage—they *go to pilot*. A pilot is just like a *television series* except that it only happens *once*. Despite this it is presented as a *world premiere*.

Several people are involved in the deal. They include the person who *packages* the idea, known as the *producer;* the representative of the studio or network, known as the *executive;* sometimes a writer, known as *replaceable;* the agent, known as *Mel;* and the person who thought up the idea in the first place, known to the writer as the *writer,* to the producer as the *producer,* and so forth. These people tend to meet for lunch, known as the *deduction*.

At this deduction, the parties involved *compliment* each other on how much they like each other's work.

Shortly after this point the deal will start to *fall apart,* generally due to something called the *unavailability* of someone called *Redford*. Now the parties will call each other *things which can't be repeated here*. It becomes the responsibility of the executive to see that the others will *never work in this Industry again*.

Some months later it is customary for one of the parties to the Deal to call another for a conciliation session, known as *tennis*. At this session another deal is considered. This deal will also involve availability—this time of someone known to everyone as *Larry,* except in that person's presence, where he is known as *Lord Olivier*.

Meanwhile the original Deal has done something known as *going into turnaround*. This means that whoever had the idea first, or whoever *bought the idea* from that person, is free to try selling the idea, which is known as *shopping the idea*. In order to make the idea appear fresh and desirable it may be necessary to alter the original idea, making (for instance) a dramatic romance set in the court of Louis XIV into a science-fiction comedy set in prehistoric Japan. This is known as *a few small changes*.

While this project is brewing, Larry has become unavailable, making that other project *come unattached*. At this point one of the parties will have a minor idea, known as an *inspiration*. *Both projects can be combined into one.* They are then expanded well beyond the two hours required to tell whatever *story* they had, and this is called a *miniseries*. If the miniseries spawns a book, or *novelization,* or even just enough publicity, it is no longer just a miniseries but a *media event*.

And if this production runs on television, and if it runs for more than three nights and people still stay up to watch it, then all the parties to the deal are motivated to fight for credit for the project, now referred to by each as *my baby*. And for the person who wins this power struggle, known as *friendship,* comes the right to be called by Hollywood's greatest accolade: *genius.*

Life-at-a-Glance

Since life in The Industry is an endless string of meetings punctuated by phone calls (or perhaps vice versa), you will need some way of keeping track of your appointments and contacts. Your secretary can keep track of some of this information, but much of your day will be spent in transit. Thus, everyone in The Industry is automatically issued an Eaton At-A-Glance appointment book, generally the medium-size week-or-day-at-a-glance variety. This you will carry everywhere, except into the Jacuzzi, where you should leave it on a chair within reach. For many of you, the week-at-a-glance will be your only real office.

Are You Someone or Are You Just a Type?

HOW TO BE LIKE A STAR:

1. Avoid paparazzi, especially when they're not there. Walk into restaurants very rapidly and with great self-assurance—never hesitate. When a flashbulb goes off in public, turn away and half cover your face with your hand. This is the please-no-photos pose, and it makes people wonder who you are.

2. Sunglasses at night. If you want to be recognized, draw attention to the notion that you are trying *not* to be recognized.

3. Always introduce yourself by your full name. Everyone else in California uses first names only, but a star would never want to appear as if he or she *expected* you to recognize him. Thus, "Hello, I'm Jane Fonda."

4. Make restaurant reservations by stating your name first, then telling the restaurant how many people and what time. Never just call and say, "Hi, do you have a table at eight o'clock?" The star approach results in one of three things happening. The maître d' assumes that since you sound as though you expect your name to be recognized you must be somebody important and gives you the table you want; the maître d' mistakenly assumes that he does know who you are and gives you the table you want; the maître d' assumes you are a nut and gives you the table you want because he doesn't want any trouble.

5. Pay people to approach you and ask for autographs. Decline politely.

6. Dress like a slob in fancy places. Who but a star would try to get away with that?

7. Refer all requests—for jobs, dates, handouts, anything—to your agent.

8. Practice these phrases for use in stores:
   a. Give me one in every color.
   b. Do you deliver to the Malibu Colony?
   c. I don't seem to have brought any cash or credit cards.
   d. I could use those in my next project. Could you knock off, say, fifty percent?
   e. Is anyone else going to be wearing this to the Oscars?

9. Leave your car in front of wherever you are, whether there's a parking space, a valet, or neither.

10. Don't wait for the security guard at the studio gate to look for your pass. Wave breezily and drive right on through.

11. Kiss everybody.

SPECIAL ACKNOWLEDGMENTS

I would like to thank Warren Beatty, Barbra Streisand, Jon Peters, Meryl Streep, Mr. and Mrs. James Stewart, Patrick Terrail, Jose Eber, Steven Spielberg, Liza Minnelli, Marlon Brando, everybody at ICM and at the Beverly Hills Hotel, John Z. DeLorean, the cast of *Dynasty,* Jack Nicholson, and numerous others too small to mention, without whom this section of the book would have been impossible.

J.R.

REAL MOVIE EXEC

nineteen years old
sneakers
carrying Week-At-A-Glance
gold Rolex
sweat shirt

REAL RECORD EXEC

carrying Week-At-A-Glance
English teacher look
knit tie
backstage pass
cowboy boots

WARNING: THE FOLLOWING ARE NOT REAL EXECUTIVES, BUT IMPOSTORS. DO NOT SLEEP WITH THEM.

PHONY MOVIE EXEC

fat, bald
cigar
showgirl on each arm
pinky ring
gold Rolex

PHONY RECORD EXEC

satin jacket
coke spoon
cowboy boots
designer jeans
no backstage pass ("lost it")

Week 11

LANGUAGE LAB

*T*he specialized words and expressions of Southern
California are easy to understand if you remember that most of
them fall into three categories of meaning. They tend to mean
either
1. "great," "fantastic," "terrific"
or 2. "intense" or "intensely"
or 3. "very"
This rule alone speaks volumes about the sunny and enthusiastic
dispositions and speech patterns of Southern Californians.

The sources given for the words, such as **Val** (the San
Fernando Valley), **Bev. Hls.** (Beverly Hills), or surf (surf) are not
the only provinces in which these terms are used or understood;
there is much mixing and influencing. Many Valley expressions,
for instance, come from the sworn enemies of Vals, surfers.

Pronunciation is tough to convey in a book. Certain models
may be found in other media. Laraine Newman, in the Saturday

Night Live *reruns, provides some good role models; whenever she plays a particularly airheaded character, she tends to revert to either a general Southern California accent or a Valley voice.*

Remember to smile when you speak Californian, no matter what you are saying.

actor, *n.* (Hlwd.): waiter.

amped, *adj.:* enthusiastic.

awesome, *adj.* (surf, Val): great, terrific, intense.

bio, *adj.* (Bev. Hls. kids): good, great.

bitchin', *adj.* (Val): fantastic (used to describe a person, place, thing, or condition of little or no merit or value beyond the San Fernando Valley; e.g., a new headband, Zuma Beach).

casa, *n.:* **1.** *Spanish,* house, home. **2.** *So/Cal English,* honorary title believed to bring good fortune to a place of business; e.g., Casa di Cadillac, Casa de Cleaners.

cazh (also cas), *adj. or interjection:* **1.** (Val) attractive, or desirable; used (as are most terms of praise in the Valley) of possessions; e.g., cars, clothing. **2.** (Bev. Hls.) okay, sure, yes; as in *Mother: Will you and Brad go pick up the Alfa at the shop? Son: I'm cazh.*

ciao (pronounced *chow*), *salutation:* **1.** (Italian) good-bye. **2.** (Hlwd.) good-bye aren't I hip?

C.P.F., *n.* Close Personal Friend. Used by anyone in The Industry to describe anyone else in The Industry.

didge, *n.:* money, expense, cost, price (from *digits*); as in *The Lamborghini is a high-didge* (i.e., expensive) *car.*

dude (pronounced *dewd*), *n.:* **1.** (Val) guy, male person. **2.** (surf) friend, pal; always used in the greeting *Hey, dude!;* this salutation may be used for anyone from your close friends to the traffic officer who just pulled you over.

What to Name the Southern California Baby

Your child's name should be a clean, crisp, creative, distinctive name that is skillfully conceived to exaggerate femininity or masculinity, depending. Thus:

GIRLS' NAMES

The "lovely" names:
Stacy
Vanessa
Jennifer
Tiffany
et cetera, or

THE ULTIMATE FULLY POPULAR ALL-AMERICAN SOUTHERN CALIFORNIA GIRL'S NAME

Melissa

BOYS' NAMES

The fifties macho movie star names:
Troy
Lance
Erik
Kent
et cetera, or

THE ALL-TIME GRADE-A NUMBER ONE SOUTHERN CALIFORNIA BOY'S NAME

Brad

dyno, *adj.* (surf): **1.** great, terrific. **2.** high-powered, exciting.

for sure (pronounced *fer sher*), *interjection* (Val): **1.** Yes, definitely, I agree. **2.** Don't bother me, I'm not paying attention.

full on, *adj., adv.* (surf): very.

fully, *adj., adv.* (Val, Bev. Hls.): very.

give good, *v.* (Hlwd.): to use, perform, or conduct (something) with particular grace, style, or finesse; e.g., to *give good phone*, to *give good book*. The object of the phrase must always be in the singular.

GUD, *abbrv.:* Geographically UnDesirable. Used to refer to dates who live too far away to make the drive worth the effort. Thus, to be branded GUD is the modern equivalent, in social terms, of Hester Prynne's big red *A.*

gnarly, *adj.* (surf): **1.** intense, extreme, possibly dangerous. **2.** great, terrific, fantastic. **3.** awful.

go for it, *v.:* **1.** to do (something), especially with some enthusiasm or vigor. **2.** To do (something) without much vigor while trying to give the *impression* of enthusiasm.

hamburger, *n.:* any of a variety of food preparations, each of which must contain at least a grilled patty of chopped beef, a bread bun, lettuce, tomato, and onion, with mayonnaise or Russian or Thousand Island dressing; and which may contain cheese or sprouts.

Have a good one!, *salutation:* Good-bye. (Originally, a euphemism for *Have a nice day!*)

Have a nice day!, *salutation:* **1.** Good-bye! **2.** the state motto of Southern California.

Hi!, *salutation:* the other state motto of Southern California.

hot, *adj.:* **1.** good, great, terrific. **2.** enthusiastic. **3.** (used of clothes) fashionable (though probably silly-looking). **4.** sexually attractive (used to promote network TV stars).

The Industry, *n.* (Hlwd.): **1.** any or all of the movie, television, or music businesses. **2.** also used to describe any ancillary business, especially in singles bars. Thus, restaurateurs, waiters, hair stylists, letter carriers, mechanics, and so on, any portion of whose clientele is derived from the movie, television, or recording industries, may claim to work "in The Industry."

kill, *adj.* (Bev. Hls. kids): great, terrific. That's right, it's used as an adjective. Thus, *a kill pair of pants.*

SAMPLE CONVERSATION NUMBER 1: THE ROSE CAFÉ, VENICE

NONA: So you're allowing him to give energy to you. . . .
LHASA: No, *it's given me great meaning.*
NONA: Oh, I see. Can I buy you a tea?
LHASA: Do they have herb teas?
NONA: I'll ask. Waiter, what kind of tea do you have?
WAITER: We have Red Zinger, Sleepytime, Mandarin Orange Spice, Cinnamon Rose, Iced Delight, Earl Grey, Darjeeling . . .
LHASA: I'll have the Red Zinger. And a chocolate croissant.
NONA: Where did you get those leg warmers?
LHASA: A woman in my ashram makes them. I have a pair to match each outfit.
NONA: So you were saying something about great meaning. . . .
LHASA: Yes. My life has been transformed.
NONA: I thought it was transformed last month, at the retreat.
LHASA: It was. This is different.

Ten Conversational Gambits for Talk Shows

1. "I don't care a hoot about the Oscars. Sure, I'll be happy if I win one, but it's the *work* that I love."

2. "Oh, Merv, you're too kind. You embarrass me."

3. "Really? You have a clip from my movie? What a nice surprise!"

4. "In this scene I'm trying to deal with my grief because my puppy has just been shot, then I escape by swinging from a burning rope that's dangling from a helicopter and then I make love to Sigourney Weaver."

5. "You want me to *sing*? But I don't have anything prepared. Well, okay."

6. "It's not that I don't believe in *marriage,* it's that I don't believe in marriage as an *institution*."

7. "During the break you were asking what it was like working with Olivier. Well, it was a privilege. A privilege and an honor.

Olivier is the greatest. No—that's okay—you can applaud. It's for Olivier."

8. "I only gained all this weight because the role called for it."

9. "I just came back from China (or Israel or Egypt or Africa). China ... is fantastic. You've been, haven't you?"

10. "Let me tell you what the difference is between New York and L.A."

First-Name Basis

In Southern California your first name is all you will need in over ninety-seven percent of all social and business situations.

All introductions at parties are made thus:

"Chuck, this is Dina. Dina, this is Chuck."

If two people have the same first name, the introduction is like this:

"Chuck, this is Chuck. Chuck, this is Chuck."

Restaurant reservations are made the same way. Hence the announcement,

"Chuck party of eight."

Non–Southern Californians are frequently embarrassed when they use their customary forms of introduction in the Southland.

"Hello, I'm Marybeth MacDonald."

"Hi, Marybeth. I'm Chuck."

All the really important people are known by their first name all over the country, anyway. Liz. Dick. Liza. Merv. Johnny. Warren. Sammy.

Remember, if God had meant us to use last names, He would have used one Himself.

The Single Most Useful Phrase Available to Writers, Directors, Actors, and Other Creative Types Wishing to Shut Up Meddlesome Production Executives

"We tried it that way but it didn't work."

killer, *adj.* (surf): great, terrific, intense. Used especially of drugs and waves.

Let's do it!, *expression:* Let's get out of here; Let's leave.

mellow out, *v.:* **1.** relax **2.** (when used in the imperative) Shut up!

not even, (pronounced *not eeeven!*): no; never; uh-uh; definitely not; no way, Jay.

-n't, *suffix* (Val): used sarcastically to negate a preceding phrase; thus, *It was pretty good . . . n't?*

Amy God!, *exclamation,* (Val); the universal term of excitement of the young San Fernando Valley woman. The correct pronunciation is to linger on the first syllable, to make a mad dash through the second, and to raise the voice sharply to an excruciating squeal on the final syllable. Actually spelled *"Omigod!"* but never pronounced that way.

out here, *n.,* Southern California. Used by Southern Californians when speaking to non–Southern Californians; e.g., "You know, we do have newspapers out here."

pass on, v.: **1.** (outside California) die (emph. on "on") **2.** (So/Cal., esp. Hlwd.) say no; refuse; turn down; e.g., *We're going to pass on your script; I'll pass on a date with you* (emph. on "pass").

rad (also, *radical*), *adj.,* (surf, Val, youth): exciting, intense, high-energy, dangerous. Used esp. to describe certain sports and athletic pursuits including the far fringes of surfing, skating, skateboarding, bicycling, and so on.

really (pronounced "rully"), *conversational filler:* **1.** yeah; go on; keep talking. **2.** I agree thoroughly.

Saudi prince, *n.* (Bev. Hls.): Iranian student.

shred, *v.* (surf): **1.** to surf intensely, thus, **2.** to do anything intensely.

so I'm all, *phrase:* so I said; as in "So I'm all, 'I did not!'; so he's all, 'Yes you did!' "

the Southland, *n.* When used in Southern California this means "Southern California," and not Dixie. Thus, not the Southland that will rise again but the one that may well sink.

stoked, *adj.:* enthusiastic, excited, possessed of a go-for-it attitude.

take, *v.* (Hlwd.): go to, participate in, as in "take a lunch," "take a meeting," "take a funeral."

thrashed, *adj.* (surf): intensely damaged, as by fighting, by exhaustion, by recreational drugs; also *v.,* to thrash.

totally, *conversational filler* (Val): a phrase devoid of all meaning, used as a retort in all conversation by San Fernando Valley teen-agers; It is believed that at one time the word "totally" was used to convey eager agreement and enthusiasm, and as a general intensifier, like *very*, but this meaning is largely obsolete today.

Toy, n. (always used in the expression "my new toy"): Any of a variety of expensive, brand-new, personal possessions, usually highly refined technically, and always inappropriate for child's play, despite the term *toy;* e.g., a new Ferrari, Rolex, car phone, Jacuzzi, food processor, screening room.

wasn't, *v.* (Val): was, and was very much so. Used by adolescent females going through their "ironic" phase; e.g., "Her dad came home and he *wasn't* drunk...." Similar usage includes "didn't;" e.g., "... and her mom *didn't* throw a lamp at him."

way, *adv.* (surf): very, a lot; e.g., "way cool," "way tired," "way gnarly," or "way blitzed."

you-don't-even-know: (Val) literally, "it wasn't intense," or "it was awesome," as in "We went cruising in her dad's Alfa Spider and you-don't-even-know." Pronounced like one word, with heavy emphasis on *know.*

The Standardized California Pop Quiz

There are some questions that you should be prepared to answer in any part of the country: How ya doin'? What's happenin'? D'ja see the game? Say, how about this weather?

And then there are some questions that are special to Southern California. So that you will be prepared with ready answers for *these* questions—which you *will* be asked sooner or later—here is a chance to practice.

Q: Who's your guru? **A:**_____

Q: Have you done the training? (Or, for outsiders, Have you taken est?) **A:**_____

Q: What's your sign? **A:**_____

Q: How many miles do you run? **A:**_____

Q: Who does your hair? **A:**_____

Q: Who does your house? **A:**_____

Q: Who's your agent? **A:**_____

Q: Who's your agent in New York? **A:**_____

Q: Do you have a machine (i.e., answering machine)? **A:**_____

Q: What do you drive? **A:**_____

Q: Do you know a good day worker? **A:**_____

Q: Is that (or, are those) real? **A:**_____

Q: Do you have any vitamin E (or whatever) here? **A:**_____

Q: What drugs do you do? **A:**_____

Q: How much do you make? **A:**_____

(In this last case it is permissible—even preferable—to provide the answer before the question is asked.)

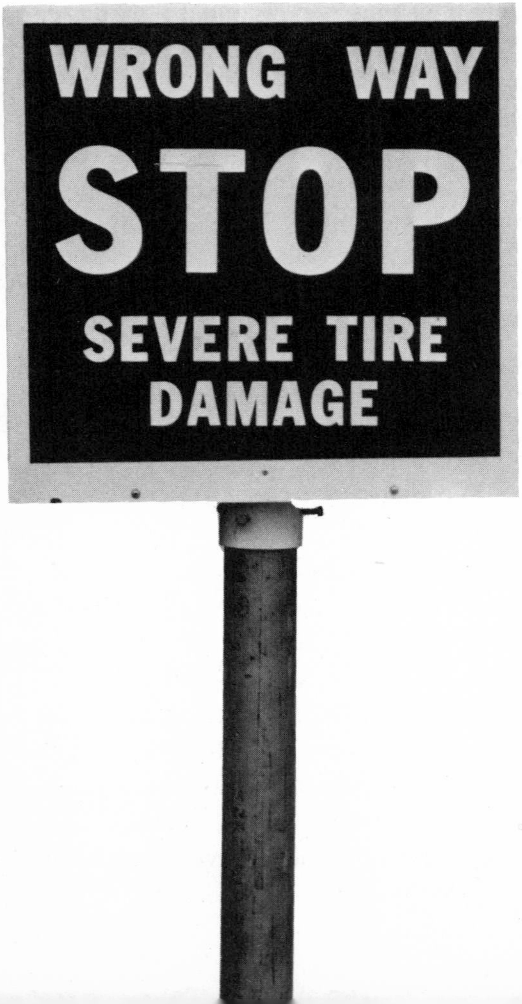
WRONG WAY
STOP
SEVERE TIRE
DAMAGE